Zohar - The Book of
Radiance Revealed

Zohar - The Book of Radiance Revealed

Dr. Robert H. Schram

Copyright © 2014 by Dr. Robert H. Schram.

ISBN:	Softcover	978-1-4931-6695-4
	Ebook	978-1-4931-6696-1

All rights reserved. No part of this book may be reproduced or transmitted in any form or by any means, electronic or mechanical, including photocopying, recording, or by any information storage and retrieval system, without permission in writing from the copyright owner.

This book was printed in the United States of America.

Rev. date: 01/28/2014

To order additional copies of this book, contact:
Xlibris LLC
1-888-795-4274
www.Xlibris.com
Orders@Xlibris.com
539692

CONTENTS

INTRODUCTION 7
SEFIROT 33
PROPHETS 68
DEMONS, DEVILS, SATAN, EVIL 72
NUMBERS, COLORS, HEBREW LETTERS AND WORDS 88
CHARACTERS—FROM CREATION THROUGH 1200 CE 112
PLACES/THINGS—GARDEN OF EDEN,
    MACHPELAH, BABEL, CLOUD, FLOOD 148
ANGELS 169
CIRCUMCISION, SOULS, REINCARNATION,
    AND RESURRECTION 180
CONCLUDING THOUGHTS 200
REFERENCES 205
GLOSSARY OF HEBREW AND OTHER WORDS 223

INTRODUCTION

There are numerous books written about Jewish mysticism, kabbalah, and the Zohar (Book of Radiance). The Zohar is written in code through the use of symbolism, euphemisms, figures of speech, ancient phraseology, and the Hebrew Bible or *Tenakh*. *Tenakh* is an acronym formed from the initial Hebrew letters of Masoretic Text's three traditional subdivisions (*Torah*—the Five Books of Moses, *Nevi'im*—Prophets, and *Ketuvim*—writings). Thanks to the incredible scholarship of Professor Daniel Matt from Berkeley California the codes of the Zohar have become more comprehensible to the inquisitive reader. It was because of Professor Matt's translation, explanations, and notes on the Zohar in his first seven volumes that I was moved to write this book. "The Zohar is firmly rooted in tradition but thrives on discovery."[1]

Comprehension of mystical traditions takes dedication and perseverance but the more meaningful and powerful impact is being able to feel its full heartfelt effects. There are a number of meditations and prayers toward this end.

> Now the time has come to elevate you in the stages of love so that you become beloved on high and delightful here on earth. First, begin by combining the letters of the name YHVH (Hebrew letters that comprise G-d's name). Gaze at all its combinations. Elevate it. Turn it over like a wheel which goes round and round, backwards and forwards like a scroll. Do not leave it aside except when you observe that it is becoming too much for you because of the confused movements in your imagination. Leave it for a while and you will be able to return to it later. You can then make your request of it and when you attain wisdom do not forsake it. For the initial letters and the final letters, the numerical values, the *notarikons*, the combination of letters and their permutations, their accents and the forms they assume, the knowledge of their names and the grasping of their ideas, the changing of many words into one and one into many, all these belong to the authentic tradition of the prophets. By means of these G-d will answer when you call upon Him for you belong to His

family. And now, my son, the secret of the L-rd is with them that fear Him and to them will He make His covenant known. He will make known His covenant to the man who fears Heaven and whose covenant is perfect. Otherwise, He will hide it, for honor is not fitting for the fool.[2]

The mystical secrets come from G-d and are impossible for anyone to impart . . . it is a matter of discovery for those who seek the essence of divinity. He was, is, will be, and is the ground root of all worlds. "This cannot be imparted to another but each man has his own degree of comprehension of the divine in proportion to his degree of understanding and manner in which it is assessed in his heart." A person who strives to better his character and puts effort into comprehending the hidden the greater will be his chances for refining his intellectual understanding. Each person's grasp of the mystery is in proportion to one's efforts and the refinement of one's spiritual nature. "The secret of the L-rd is with them that fear Him." (Psalms 25:14) Those that are in great fear of the L-rd may attain a too profound comprehension of the being of G-d and are then unable to reveal the secrets of his/her heart to others. An interpreter of lesser spiritual rank may be required to impart what he has been told to others so they can understand.[3]

Louis Jacobs beautifully explains comprehending the hidden by a parable having to do with the idea of love:

> A man is in prison where he has sat so long in darkness that he is unaware that there is any such thing as light. Adjacent to his prison is a room in which there shines a brilliant light. Suddenly a small aperture is opened and he sees the light. Or the illustration can be given of a man who is locked up in a low and dark dungeon. Near the dungeon is a huge precipice and on the precipice a high wall. Beyond this wall are further walls and beyond these a great and awesome palace containing many residences. Beyond all these residences is a house in which there shines a great and wonderful light, immeasurable and incomprehensible. This house is surrounded by many walls and that hidden light can only shine through the crevices and spaces. The light shines more brightly the nearer one is to the house, and near the outer wall the light is not at all bright. Yet even this light is most powerful when compared with the darkness of the dungeon. There are doors and windows through which it beams indirectly. It can happen that a certain door or window is opened in such a way as to beam the light directly

onto the man who dwells in darkness and he then experiences great joy. He then longs to escape from the dark dungeon in order to climb the precipice. At times of great rejoicing and celebration a tiny aperture is opened (in the house) which beams the light directly. Even though the light which comes through this aperture is as nothing compared to the light which shines through the open doors, yet since it shines directly on the recipients a great and holy illumination is theirs. When a man is worthy of seeing this light his soul longs and is set on fire without limit until he feels that he is about to expire (in ecstasy). In his great longing he risks his life to break open the door of his dungeon and springs energetically to enjoy the light. But as soon as he emerges (from the dungeon) the light is concealed and there he stands at the foot of the precipice which he is unable to climb because his limbs ache and the precipice is so steep and high. A man at the top of the precipice then lowers a ladder down to him. But it is very difficult to ascend by means of this ladder for agility is needed and willingness to risk one's neck by missing the step. He tries to ascend on the ladder but no sooner does he manage to climb a short way up then he falls back again. This occurs again and again until the L-ord of the manor has pity on him and he reaches down to grasp his right hand so that he can pull him up. The application of this parable is very profound and it is impossible to explain it in full but those in need of it will understand. See the holy work of *Sha'arei Gan Eden (Derekh Emet, I:7)* and the prayer book of Rabbi Koppel at the beginning of the intentions for the Sabbath and you will understand. This is the meaning of "Open to me, my sister," etc. "My beloved put in his hand," etc. "But my beloved turned away," etc. (Song 5:2-6) and the whole of that chapter. If you have understood the parable you will grasp the meaning of all these verses.[4]

A fool who has the light revealed to him and then has it concealed imagines that it will never be revealed again and experiences the darkness even more intensely then before seeing the light. The intelligent person questions why such a thing happened to him/her: why was such a light revealed to me? "It probably means that the L-rd of the manor is hinting to me that if I try hard enough it is within my power and my capacity to attain to the holiness of that light."

Our Jewish masters created the tradition whereby there are two types of counsel for whoever wishes to escape from the deep and dark dungeon. The first is that s/he should cry to Him/Her to bring him/her out of this darkness, until the L-rd of the manor takes pity and beams a light onto him/her so that s/he can see the way to escape. This is the way of pity. The second way is to yearn constantly for the light and to engage in contemplation on the greatness and wonder of the precipice and the great and awesome palace and the marvelous light within it. The light in the second tradition is a spiritual one and the thoughts and yearning are also of a spiritual nature. Spirit calls to spirit so that when a person's soul yearns to serve our Creat-r and when the L-rd of the manor observes how powerful is the person's longing, then, even though that person is not really worthy of it, S/He elevates the person to reach a category of that light in proportion to his/her understanding of holiness.

"And the angel of the L-rd appeared unto him in a flame of fire out of the midst of a bush . . . but the bush was not consumed." (Exodus 3:2) The holy Rabbi Ze'ev of Zbarazh expounds the verse to say that even though the bush is not consumed and is still full of evil character traits the L-rd appears there if there is 'a flame of fire,' namely, yearning and longing. Reflecting on these words can lead to the discovery of paths and encouragements for the worship of G-d. This discovery only applies when a person digs deep into the recesses of his heart in order to recognize Him/Her at whose word the world came into being. With limited effort 'The fool walketh in darkness' (Ecclesiastes 2:14) and 'A fool hath no delight in understanding.' (Proverbs 18:2) That is to say, in repentance from the depth of his heart. The fool knows nothing of how remote he is from the L-rd but s/he imagines s/he is near and that s/he knows all.[5]

The true mystic sense of awareness appreciates the majestic scale of the universe in wonder and transcendence. One can get a glimpse of this wonder by being able to suspend the dialogue in one's mind. Knowledge and appreciation can stimulate this feeling, which has a name in Hebrew: *yirah*. Jewish mystics call *yirah* the awe, or fear, of *Hashem* (G-d). The word can be used for either awe or fear and has both verbal and nominative forms. King David's psalms say, using two constructions of the word *yirah*: "I will fear (*irah*) no evil" (Psalm 23:4), and "Taste and see that G-d is good . . . Nothing is lacking to those who are in awe (*y-irah-v*)." (Psalm 34:9-10)[6]

". . . if G-d creates with language, then words themselves have significance beyond their plain meanings." The order of the letters in words may be transposed in an effort to decipher hidden or multiple implications. In Kabbalistic literature, and especially in the imagery of Isaac Luria, the first word of the

Torah is unpacked to mean many things at once: *B'Resheit:* In the beginning (i.e., of time itself). *B'Resheit:* With the dot named *Resheit*. *B'reit Esh* (rearranging the Hebrew letters): literally, in a covenant of fire. *Shir Ta'eb* (again rearranging the letters): literally, a song of desire. *Bre Sheit* (and again rearranging the letters): literally, He created from nothing, six (referring to the days or stages of creation, excluding the Sabbath). At the beginning of time, the universe was created from nothing in a series of stages initiated by an intentional act of desire or will, with a burst of conventional fire expanding dramatically outward from a microscopic point called the *Resheit*.[7]

In humanity's unending effort to understand our universe we have discovered in science what our enlightened ancestors knew through Divine connection. In subatomic physics the fourth and last of the forces is called the weak force, because it can exert influence only about a hundredth of the influence of the strong force. In the case of two adjacent protons, the effect of the weak force is about one ten-millionth that of the strong force. The weak force controls how particles decay into other particles, particularly in processes during which ghost-like particles called neutrinos are produced. The weak force may be unfamiliar to most people, but it is far from unimportant. The fusion of hydrogen into helium, for example, involves the conversion of hydrogen nuclei (single protons) into helium nuclei (two protons and two neutrons), with the resulting release of neutrinos. This is the process that powers our Sun. The weak force thus helps enable the Sun and other normal stars to shine. As written in Genesis at the earliest moments of Creation we get glimpses that the weak force and neutrinos, played a crucial role.[8]

Learning through physics what the Torah has alluded to is becoming more and more enchanting. The earth and the universe are almost exclusively made up of 'normal matter'; very little antimatter seems to exist which is fortunate since when particles of these opposite types come into contact, they annihilate each other, turning into a short burst of light—two photons—whose combined energy is related to the total mass of the two particles by Einstein's equation $E=mc^2$. The mutual annihilation of matter and antimatter illustrates the essential feature that matter can transmute into energy. During the creation of the universe (but also in laboratory situations) the reverse also occurs; energy can transform into matter. The name given to the creation of two opposite particles of matter from pure energy is pair production, and this process played a critical role in the early universe.[9]

> The visible matter—the stars, nebulae, and galaxies—constitutes a mere two percent of all the matter in the universe. The dominant contribution comes from the mysterious, non-nuclear 'dark matter' whose presence is inferred from the movements of galaxies. Whatever that dark matter is, its gravitational pull adds to that of the visible and invisible nuclear matter, and together they all contribute to slowing down the expansion of the universe.[10]

Dark matter is a good example of the more we discover and learn the further we seem to be from understanding the Divine mysteries of the universe.

> It is not bread alone that sustains the human being, but rather everything that proceeds from the Divine sustains a human being (Deuteronomy 8:3) . . . in the words of Rabbi Abraham Isaac Kook, 'One of the great afflictions of man's spiritual world is that every discipline of knowledge, every feeling, impedes the emergence of the other. The result is that most people remain limited and one-sided . . . This defect cannot continue permanently. Man's nobler future is destined to come when he will develop to a sound spiritual state so that instead of each discipline

negating the other, all knowledge, all feeling will be envisioned from any branch of it. This is precisely the true nature of reality.'[11]

In the beginning as the universe expanded (in physics called the big bang), it cooled, and as the temperature decreased, the four forces gradually differentiated from one another. Various elementary particles condensed out of the hot plasma in a sequence that might be thought of as their 'freezing points.' In the sequence the interactions between them became less and less energetic and there were mergers into other particles (or, ultimately atoms). Approximately speaking, there are four broad hierarchical periods of time in the history of the cosmos. Planck time (named after Max Planck, the founder of quantum mechanics) is the earliest time in the universe physicists can model with any confidence. It is suspected that at some early time, possibly earlier than the Planck time, gravity assumed an identity separate from the other three forces.

The second period spans from the end of the Planck time through the dramatic moment about 10-35 seconds later, when the strong force became distinct from the weak and electromagnetic forces. This event, called the 'symmetry breaking' between the forces, led to the exponential inflation of the universe and the eventual production of matter.

The third period began with the end of inflation and lasted for about three hundred thousand years. It featured the sequential preeminence of quarks, leptons, radiation, and finally atomic nuclei.

The final period is characterized by neutral matter and commenced when temperatures in the universe had cooled to only a few thousand degrees, allowing neutral atoms to exist. This era has lasted 13.7 billion years so far. It is distinguished by the production of galaxies, stars, and finally—life. Each of these four hierarchical periods corresponds to one of the four kabbalistic worlds.[12]

> The Lurianic Kabbalists emphasized that the process of the Creation, which originated as a formless expansion, necessarily involved the aspects of shaping, constriction, and limitation. The Zohar says, 'When the most secret of secrets sought to be revealed, He made first of all a single point, and this became thought. He made all the designs there; He did all the engravings there, and He engraved within the hidden holy luminary an engraving of hidden design . . . the beginning of construction.'[13]

In mathematics the results of construction have been discovered by the work of Benoit Mandelbrot, Edward Lorenz, and others. One can create a series of points by interacting or computing a rather simple formula over and over again. Because of the nature of the formula, the data changes ever so slightly each time it is computed. When the resulting points from computing the formula are plotted, shapes which appear organic result. Later versions used by plotting seemingly random data came out looking like mountain ranges and other natural phenomena when plotted as mathematical diagrams. But this was only part of the story. Mathematicians soon realized that if one looked at any piece of the entire shape, at any level of scale or magnification, the original shapes were essentially repeated at that new level, over and over again. For example if a little section of a squiggly line is magnified, it will not resolve itself into a new shape—such as a straight line—but will look very much like the original squiggly line. When magnified again and again the same thing will happen. These fractal shapes, then, have self-similarity on all levels of scale. It is like peering into ever-smaller pieces of infinity.

This principle of self-similarity indicates that there is a connecting link between many levels of reality: the universe—from the spiral of galaxies to the spiral of DNA, from the kidney's branchlike structures to the folds in the brain. It seems as if all of reality is trying to express some similar, fundamental idea through many levels of creation.[14]

Science has accumulated many insights about the concept of free will. The laws of physics are known, and even were they not known, they nevertheless would still exist. Physics specifies with incredible precision how a system, even a very complicated one with vast numbers of particles, will evolve over time. Predicting what will happen in the future is accomplished by determining a system's initial conditions and allowing the laws of physics (through simple cause and effect) to propagate the system and determine what happens next. We may not be intelligent to know or figure out the future, but by the laws of physics everything is predetermined by the rules. By the rules of physics free will is an illusion.[15]

If everything is predetermined by the rules as science claims why study and strive to know our Divine Creat-r? It is in our nature to seek and know G-d because *Hashem* is not separate from us. He is our innermost tissue . . . our closer-than-closest self and we desire to know ourselves and understand the world and universe we live in, which is also G-d. We are searching for what we always have known in our heart-of-hearts . . . our Creat-r has always been and will always be. All the world's religions have been given to us from people who came before us and told and taught us what to believe. Those of us who are in touch with that inner drive to understand want to understand beyond bodily excitement and/or the struggles of living . . . we want to know directly through the metaphysical. Kabbalah and its sacred book the Zohar are the tools handed down to us from masters who understood the metaphysical aspects of G-d. These tools of understanding are available to us in the 21st century, more alive and approachable than ever before, thanks to the efforts of many modern day scholars. We only need to take the time, have the courage, and make the effort to discover and learn for ourselves.[16]

> The process of transformation can be aided by one of the methodologies of kabbalah known as *gematria,* a traditional method of Torah exegesis. *Gematria* is the science of assigning numerical values to Hebrew letters in order to reveal deep associations and meanings, seeking to make clear actual, often hidden, correspondences among ideas, insights, and even physical objects that on the surface have little obvious connection. It sees each letter as an element in a series of perspectives that are enfolded into the appearance that Reality finally takes.

Unlike most other languages, which have their origins in *Yetzirah*—that is to say, the world of symbols and associations—Hebrew has a totally consistent structure based on the briatic is-ness of the thing-in-itself. For example, in English, letters are basically symbols that stand for sounds. While the letters of the Hebrew alphabet similarly stand for sounds, each letter is also essentially linked to a condition or quality—that is, each letter is a condition or form Reality can potentially take. These 'conditions' are the building blocks out of which the universe is made. Thus the letters of the Hebrew alphabet can be seen as units of Creation, with creative potential in and of themselves.

We gain a deeper understanding of this by remembering that biology sees all life forms as being derived from the sequence of only eight basic elements. The different amino acids are created not by new chemical compounds, but by the arrangement of eight primary bases. These eight bases are responsible for the creation of all proteins, and—folded and arranged in special ways—all of the genetic code. Similarly, the infinite variety of forms in this universe can be seen as arising from the arrangement of the twenty-two letters of the Hebrew alphabet.

This implies that the individual conditions, or 'consciousness,' that corresponds to the building blocks (the letters) existed prior to the Creation of the universe. From this perspective, these 'letters' 'preexist' the creation of duality—that is, our world itself. Our world, ourselves, all, spring from this fountain.

Thus the first letter of the Hebrew alphabet *aleph*, stands for such conditions as unity, power, stability, and continuity. This is true in all cases; every word that contains an *aleph* has these conditions embedded in the essence of that thing or action.

The second letter, *bet* embodies the conditions of interiority, of dwelling, as in dwelling in a house. It is the place primal energy can dwell. In Hebrew, every word that has interiority as its main preoccupation contains a *bet*.

As an example, we can look at the first word of Genesis, *bereshit*, which begins in Hebrew with the letters *bet* and *resh* (the twentieth letter of the Hebrew alphabet). While the aforementioned *bet* exemplifies interiority, *resh* exemplifies movement, the head, or the beginning of a new enterprise. Fabre d'Olivet, the author of the seminal nineteenth-century work 'The Hebraic Tongue Restored,' likens *resh* to the radius of a circle that produces the circumference. So *resh* is the figure of potential creation. In this way, the first word of Genesis takes on new meaning. If we drop associative thinking and, in the Pure Present, consider this word, we actually begin to feel the power it has and its place in creation. In other words, the word has power within itself.

Because of this, *gematria* is much more than a method for finding psychological associations or poetic correspondences between different words—as valuable as that might be. The relationships exposed by *gematriac* analysis are primary, since they are, in a sense, instructions for creation rather than commentary after the fact.[17]

If we and our world spring from the same fountain then if we attack nature with our polluting methods of manufacturing and if we let the quality of life fade in the name of speed and efficiency, then symptoms may arise. Our bodies reflect or participate in the world's body, so that if we harm that outer body, our own bodies will feel the effects. Essentially there is no distinction between the world's body and the human body.

Just as men and women must be united to form a harmonious whole, disease desires to find a wife (i.e., medicine) to bring about harmony in the body. Many ancient physicians were also musicians concerned with rhythms, tonalities, discords, and concords of the body and soul. They wanted to know what was the nature of the dissonance that the patient felt as pain and discomfort?[18]

The universe has always been a very violent place. The word violence comes from the Latin word *vis*, meaning 'life force.' Its very roots suggest that in violence the thrust of life is making itself visible. If everything including us is created from stardust arranged in a myriad of ways then the 'life force' of our universe and us originates and is dependent on violence. If violence in the form of anger and rage is not present in us then our future survival is at risk since life will not go on without the Divine 'life force' within us. We are no different from the weeds that utilize its *vis* to grow up through cement no matter how many times we cut it off. If we try taming and boxing in the weeds innate power, it inevitably finds its way into the light like humans who use their *vis* to create, discover, and survive.[19]

According to Samuel the Small our world resembles the human eyeball. The sclera (white) is the ocean. The iris (black) is the inhibited world. The pupil is Jerusalem and the reflection of one's own face seen in the pupil of another person's eye is the Temple.

> The land of Israel sits in the center of the world, Jerusalem in the center of the land of Israel, the Temple in the center of Jerusalem, the nave in the center of the Temple, the ark in the center of the nave, and in front of the ark is the Stone of Foundation, from which the world was founded. Zion refers to the site of the Temple, within which dwells *Shekhinah* (the settling of the Divine presence on earth). She reflects all of the other *sefirot* (G-d's emanations on earth) and includes within Herself images of all being.[20]

Through the eye the son inherits the world from his father because of the eye's cosmic symbolism and, more simply, because sight yields perception and knowledge.[20]

The Zohar is a mystical, often an ecstatic work, or at least one in which the ecstatic dimension is very highly developed. A very strong expression of this ecstasy is in the Zohar's powerful and poetic soliloquies around the word *Zohar* itself, and on the verse (Daniel 12:3) from which the work's title is taken: "The enlightened shall shine like the radiance (*zohar*) of the sky, and those who lead multitudes to righteousness, like the stars, forever." Zohar represents the hidden radiance issuing forth from the highest *sefirotic* realms. It is a showering of sparks lighting up all that comes in its path. "Its inspiration is surely the night sky, the wondrous event of shooting stars against the background of the Milky Way. But like all such images in mystical literature, the beacon of light or drop of divine seed is a pictorial representation of an event that takes place also within the mystic's heart, the inspiration that 'sparks' this creative vision."[21]

> The inner event of this radiant presence is outwardly manifest in the shining gaze of the kabbalist's face. 'The enlightened shall shine' is also understood in this rather literal way. Here, as frequently in the

Zohar, there is an assimilation of the kabbalist to the biblical description of Moses as he emerged from the Tent of Meeting, his face glowing with the radiant presence of G-d. But the kabbalist is also Moses' brother Aaron, the ancient priest whose face shines with divine presence as he bestows the blessing of G-d's own countenance upon the children of Israel. 'May the Lord cause His face to shine upon you' (Numbers 6:25) is seen as the Torah's personified way of calling forth the same light that the kabbalist as Neoplatonist perceives to be shining forth from one cosmic rung to another. He now seeks to become the earthly bearer of that light, transmitting it to his community of disciples and readers. This is the kabbalist (most often personified in the Zohar by Rabbi Shim'on son of Yohai) in the role of *tsaddiq*, conveyer of divine light.[21]

The great religious creativity—and even the ecstatic deaths—of Rabbi Shim'on and his disciples are meant to induce in the reader some sense that s/he too may continue on this path of knowing and feeling the Zohar's secrets. The reader may be aroused and long for such enlightenment and/or inspiration. "While no generation before the advent of messiah will fully equal that of Rabbi Shim'on, all those who come in his wake are encouraged to follow in his path. The Zohar is thus a highly evocative work, one that seeks to create and sustain a mood of ecstatic devotion." Certain biblical verses are used as awakeners or bells to "regularly restimulate awareness, rousing readers from their daily torpor and reminding them of the constant vital flow needed to quicken the cosmos." This reminder is meant to renew and refresh their participation in Israel's great collective task of rousing *Shekhinah*. She in turn awakens Her divine Lover to release the flow of light/water/seed, enveloping Her in His presence and renewing the universal flow of life."[21]

Shekhinah emerged from the womb of *Binah,* known as *Mi* (who or whom). A spiritual seeker may inquire about Her, but such questions do not yield ordinary answers. The identity of the Divine is discovered only in the realm beyond words. The mystical name 'Who' becomes a focus of meditation, as question turns into quest.[22] To enter and experience higher dimensions, the soul is enveloped in a radiant garment. The garment is woven out of one's virtuous days. Parallels appear in Islamic and Iranian eschatology—and in Mahayana Buddhism. BT Yoma 42 "Moses ascended in the cloud, was enveloped by the cloud, and was sanctified within the cloud—so as to receive Torah for Israel in holiness."[23]

Every year, as commanded by G-d, at the Passover Sedar the story of Jewish deliverance from Egyptian slavery is read in the *Haggadah* (telling, expounding). *Haggadah* corresponds with *Hokhimah* (wisdom), beyond *Binah* (understanding). In the Zohar the term *Haggadah* can refer to the allegorical interpretation of Scripture, which unlocks secrets of wisdom that cannot be expressed openly.[24]

SEFIROT

Understanding the *Sefirot* is critical to understanding kabbalah and the Zohar. The word *Shekhinah* in Hebrew represents the feminine attributes of the presence of G-d. Israel's great collective mystical task is to arouse *Shekhinah*. In turn She will awaken her divine Lover to release His flow of light/water/seed and thus renew the universal flow of life. "The 'Eden' (or Lebanon) whence that flow is to come is an accessible if hidden rung within the divine and human self." It is not an ancient and lost site in the Bible, nor is it only the paradise to which souls will ascend to after death. "Eden is the 'upper world,' a recondite and inward aspect of being that is mirrored in the 'garden,' the One who needs to be watered by that flow. We creatures of the 'lower world,' trees growing in the garden, need to trace back the course of that river to its source, linking the upper and lower worlds (*Binah* and *Shekhinah*, but also *Shekhinah* and 'this' world, or *Shekhinah* and the soul), so that the flow will never cease.[1]

The Ten Sefirot:

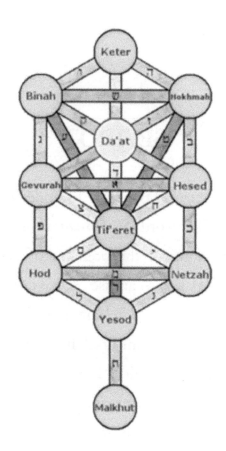

Center *Keter*—Crown, Will, *Ayin* (Nothingness)

Left *Binah*—Understanding, Palace, Womb

Right *Hokhmah*—Wisdom, Primordial Point, Beginning

Left *Gevurah*—Power, *Din* (Judgment), Rigor, Red, Fire, Left Arm, Isaac

Right *Hesed*—Love, *Gedullah* (Greatness), Grace, White, Water, Right Arm, Abraham

Center *Tif'eret*—Beauty, *Rahamim* (Compassion), Blessed Holy One, Heaven, Sun, Harmony, King, Green, Torso, Jacob, Moses

Left *Hod*—Splendor, Prophecy, Left Leg

Right *Netsah*—Endurance, Prophecy, Right Leg

Center *Yesod*—Foundation, *Tsaddiq* (Righteous One), Covenant, Phallus, Joseph

Center *Malkhut*—Kingdom *Shekhinah* (Presence), Assembly of Israel, Earth, Moon, Queen, Apple Orchard, King David, Rachel

Divine creative light in Hebrew is *sefirot,* deriving from the word for 'enumeration' (*sfr*) and the word *fro* 'declare.' In Psalm 19:2 "The heavens declare (*sfr*) the glory of G-d." Isaiah Tishby, the distinguished scholar who anthologized the Zohar texts and translated them into Hebrew, describes the *sefirot* in the following way:

> The G-d who reveals Himself through His attributes and powers is depicted (in the kabbalah) in a system of ten *sefirot* . . . In this symbolic system the *sefirot* are seen as spiritual forces, attributes of the soul, or as means of activity within the G-dhead, that is to say, as revelations of the hidden G-d, both to Himself and to that which is other than He. The fundamental

element in this revelation is His emergence from the depths of limitless infinity. The *sefirot* become specified, limited areas within the G-dhead, not, of course, limited in the sense of tangible objects, but as displaying a spiritual pattern of categories both of content and of character.[2]

The ten *sefirot* are described as being 'without concreteness' (*b'limah*, literally, 'without anything'), a descriptive expression that may be associated with the words of Job 26:7: 'He hangs the world on nothing.' In the words of thirteenth-century kabbalist Moses de Leon:

> The ten *sefirot* are the secret of existence, the array of wisdom by which the worlds above and below were created. Corresponding to this secret are the ten utterances by which the world was created . . . that is, the ten times G-d speaks in the Genesis creation narrative, from Genesis 1:1 to 1:31 (if you are counting, note that the list embraces the indirect association of speech with the first word, *B'Resheit*) . . . and the ten commandments, which epitomize the holy Torah. Indeed the ten *sefirot* constitute the secret of divine existence; they comprise above and below, every single thing. They

are ancient and concealed. From them emerges the mystery of the supernal chariot . . . a matter of concealed and sealed for those who discover knowledge.[2]

Merkavah (chariot) mysticism "designates a form of visionary mystical praxis." The practice is close to apocalyptic literature except the voyager is taken up into the heavens and usually is offered a private encounter with divine glory. To go down into *merkavah* is to seek visions before the throne of G-d and to travel through the divine 'palaces' (*heikhalot*) and realms replete with angels. At the height of ecstasy one may even participate in or lead an angelic chorus. Prophet Ezekiel's opening vision gives us the concept of *merkavah* (chariot) and links to all such visionary experiences and accounts. It is also linked to Isaiah's (6) *qedushah* formula ('Holy, holy, holy is YHVH of hosts; the whole earth is filled with His glory!') since this refrain is what "most *Merkavah* voyagers recount hearing the angels sing as they stand with them in the heavenly heights."[3]

The *sefirah Binah* at the beginning of time brought forth emanations of pure *Din* (judgment) resulting in annihilation by intense and absolute forces of destruction. The residue of the destructive forces raised a hierarchy of powers of unmitigated judgment. Ontologically these forces are dependent on divinity and have no creative potency of their own; they are energized by the power released by human transgression.

The term *sefirot* is the realm of divine entities originating in *Sefer Yetsirah*, where it refers to the ten primal numbers that, along with the twenty-two letters of the Hebrew alphabet, comprise the 'thirty-two wonderous paths of wisdom' or the essential structure of existence. It is these forces and the dynamic interplay among them that constitutes the inner life of the G-dhead. Proper worship is to know G-d and to do so one must understand the symbolic language of the *sefirot*. To be a kabbalist is to contemplate the flow of energy among the *sefirot* and relect upon their ultimate unity. The term *Ein Sof* appears as the hidden source from which the ten *sefirot* emerge. *Ein Sof* originally meant 'endlessly' and is used in a nominal sense to designate 'the Endless' or 'that which is beyond all limits.' "*Ein Sof* refers to the endless and undefinable reservoir of divinity, the ultimate source out of which everything flows. *Ein Sof* is utterly transcendent in the sense that no words can describe it, no mind comprehend it. But it is also ever-present in the sense of the old rabbinic adage 'He is the place of the world.'" Nothing can ever exist outside of *Ein Sof*. It is thus not quite accurate to say that the *sefirot* 'emerge' or 'come' out of *Ein Sof*. Of necessity the hidden reaches of infinity eludes human comprehension but there stirs a primal desire, the slightest rippling in the stillness of cosmic solitude. That desire draws the

> infinite well of energy called *Ein Sof* toward self-expression: a becoming manifest or a concretization that begins with the subtlest of steps, moves toward the emergence of G-d as divine persona, manifests its spectrum of energies in the 'fullness' of the ten *sefirot*, and then spills over with plentitude to create all the 'lower' worlds, including—as its very lowest manifestation—the material universe. The *sefirot* are thus a revelation, a rendering more accessible, of that which has existed in *Ein Sof* all along.[4]

The highest *sefirah* Keter represents the first stirrings of intent within *Ein Sof*. It is the arousal of desire that comes forth into the varied life of being. There is no specific 'content' to *Keter;* it is a desire, an intentionality, a spiritual inner movement, that potentially bears all content, but actually none. *Keter* is often designated by the kabbalists as 'Nothing.' It is a stage of reality that lies between being wholly within the One and the first flickering of separate existence. The prime pictorial image assigned to it is that of the crown: the starting point of the cosmic process. Sometimes the highest rung of being is referred to as *Keter Elyon*, the Supreme Crown of G-d. The Supreme Crown image derives partly from depicting the ten *sefirot* in anthropic form, i.e., in the image of a human being. The more primary meaning of the word *keter* is 'circle' and thus the notion of a crown. In *Sefer Yetsirah* it is written that the *sefirot* are a great circle, "their end embedded in their beginning, and their beginning in their end."

Hokhmah emerges from *Keter*, as the first and finest point of real existence. Mystical traditions love the language of paradox, a way to show how inadequate words really are to describe reality. In *kabbalah* all things, souls, and moments of time that are ever to be, exist within a primal point, at once infinitesimally small and great beyond measure. The first step of the primal process is a transition from nothingness to being, from pure potential to the first point of real existence; it is the move from *Keter to Hokhmah*. 'Wisdom comes from Nothingness.' (Job 28:12) All the variety of existence is contained within *Hokhmah*, ready to begin the journey forward.

The primordial teaching of *Hokhmah* (wisdom) represents the inner mind of G-d, the Torah that exists prior to the birth of words and letters. Truth and wisdom, like the concentrated form of being exists prior to creation. "In the beginning' as 'through Wisdom' G-d created the world. Creation and Revelation are twin processes, existence and language, the real and the nominal, emerging together from the hidden mind of G-d. *Hokhmah* symbolized by the letter *yod* (the smallest of the Hebrew letters) is the first point from which all the other letters will be written as with the primal point of existence. Ergo all of the Torah, the text and the commentary indeed all of human wisdom is contained within a single *yod*. This *yod* is the first letter of the name of G-d and the upper tip of the *yod* points toward *Keter*.

Moving from the inner divine Nothingness toward the beginning of existence inevitably arouses duality, even within the inner realms. *Hokhmah* emerges and brings forth its own mate, called *Binah*, 'understanding' or 'contemplation.' *Hokhmah* is seen as a point of light seeking a grand mirrored palace of reflection. "The light seen back and forth in those countless mirrored surfaces is all one light, but infinitely transformed and magnified in the reflective process." *Hokhmah* and *Binah* are inseparable, linked to one another. "*Hokhmah* is too fine and subtle to be detected without its reflections or reverberations in *Binah*. The mirrored halls of *Binah* would be dark and unknowable without the light of *Hokhmah*." To kabbalists they are the primal pair, the ancestral *Abba* and *Imma* (Father and Mother): the deepest polarities of male and female within the Divine (and human) Self. As primal Male and Female, the point and the palace, each are transformed and fulfilled in their union with one another. Metaphors of flowing light and water are used to describe the energy that radiates from the point of *Hokhmah*. Images of sexual union are also utilized; the flow of light is also the flow of seed that fills the womb of *Binah* and gives birth to all the further rungs within the ten-in-one divine structure, the seven 'lower' *sefirot*.

The first *sefirot* triad is quite obscure and beyond human attainment. *Binah* is the womb of existence, the jubilee in which all returns to its source, the object of *teshuvah* (turning, returning). In another words *Binah* is the highest object of the religious quest to return to the source. The Divine self as in each human personality (G-d's image in the world) is an interplay of the seven forces or inner directions (lower seven *sefirot*). G-d is the first Primal Entity to emerge out of the Divine womb, to take shape as the endless energies of *Ein Sof* begin to coalesce. The *sefirot* sequence is not related to time as we know it; it comprises the inner life of YHVH, above time and space. Intrinsic logic guides the *sefirot* sequence with each stage as a response to that which comes before it. "The structure consists of two dialectical traids (sets of thesis, antithesis, and synthesis) and a final vehicle of reception that also energizes the entire system from 'below' corresponding to *Keter* at the 'upper' end."

First to manifest is *Hesed*, the grace of love of G-d. When G-d emerges from hiding it is an act of love; an endless showering of blessing and life on all beings, each of whose birth in a sense will continue this process of emerging from the One. The gift of love has no limit and represents the boundless compassion of *Keter* transposed into a love for every form and creature that is ever to emerge. G-d embodies judgment as well as love and *Hesed* emerges linked to its opposite, described as *Din*, the judgment of G-d and *Gevurah*, the bastion of divine power. Divine wisdom understands that love alone is not the way to bring forth 'other' beings and to allow them their place. The bounteous and unlimited love of G-d, the channel of grace, is the original divine *sheaf*. *Hesed* represents the G-d of love and calls forth the love in the human soul, while *Gevurah* represents the G-d humans fear, the One before whose power we stand in trembling. Abraham, the first true follower of G-d stands parallel to *Hesed*, the first G-dly quality to emerge. Abraham is the man of love; he leaves all behind to follow G-d across the deserts, offering everything including his son, Isaac. *Gevurah* is the G-d called 'Fear of Isaac' (Genesis 31:42). It is the Divine face Isaac sees when bound on the sacrificial altar, confronting the G-d he believes is about to demand his life. Isaac's piety is of a different quality than his father's. Trembling obedience, rather than love, marks his path through life and is often depicted in the Zohar as a G-d of terror.

The marriage or linking of *Hesed* and *Gevurah* is a balance that is infinitely delicate. G*evurah* becomes impatient with *Hesed,* unwilling to see judgment set aside in the name of love. Rather than permitting love to flow in measured ways, *Gevurah* seeks for some cosmic moment to rule alone, to hold back the flow of love. In this 'moment,' divine power turns to rage or fury; out of it all the forces of evil are born, darkness emerging from the light of G-d, a shadow of the Divine universe that continues to exist throughout history, sustained by the evil wrought by humans below. Judgment not tempered by love brings about evil; power obsessed with itself turns demonic. The force of evil is *sitra ahra,* 'the other side,' indicating that it represents a parallel emanation to that of the *sefirot.* But the origin of that demonic reality that both parallels and mocks the Divine is not in some 'other' distant force. The demonic is born of an imbalance within the Divine, flowing ultimately from the same source as all else, the single source of being.

The proper balance between *Hesed* and *Gevurah* results in the sixth *sefirah* (represented by the third patriarch, Jacob also called Israel), the center of the *sefirotic* universe . . . Poised between the right and the left forces within Divinity, the 'blessed Holy One' is the key figure in a central column of *sefirot*, positioned directly below *Keter*, the divine that precedes duality . . . The perfect integration of the forces of Abraham and Isaac, the G-d who unites and balances love and fear.

> Nonpersonal designations for this sixth *sefirah* include *Tif'eret* (Beauty, Splendor), *Rahamin* (Compassion), *mishpat* (balanced judgment), and *emet* (truth). The three consonants of *emet* represent the first, middle, and the last letters of the alphabet. Truth is stretched forth across the whole of being, joining the extremes of right and left, *Hesed* and *Gevurah*, into a single integrated personality. Thus is the sixth *sefirah* also described as the central 'beam' in G-d's construction of the universe. Adopting a line from Moses' Tabernacle (Exodus 26:28), depicted by the rabbis as reflecting the cosmic structure, Jacob or the sixth *sefirah* is called 'the central beam, reaching from one end unto the other.'[4]

The 'blessed Holy One' as a personal G-d serves as a model of the idealized human persona; it is the uppermost manifestation called Israel. Each member of the house of Israel partakes of this G-dhead and may also be seen as a totemic representation of His people below. The sages believe that Jacob is a new Adam, and ergo the perfect human . . . the radiant-faced elder extending blessing through the world. By imitating G-d who stands at the center between right and left, balancing all the cosmic forces, the people of Israel can balance their own lives. G-d knows us and sees Himself in us and like Him we reflect the cosmic struggle to integrate love and judgment as a great human task. The inner structure of our psychic life is the hidden structure of the universe and we can come to know G-d by the path of inward contemplation and true self-knowledge.

The second triad of the *sefirot, Netsah, Hod* and *yesod* are arranged in the same manner as those above them. The second triad is essentially channels through which the higher energies pass on their way into the tenth *sefirah, Malkhut* or *Shekhinah,* the source of all life in the lower worlds. The only major function assigned to *Netsah* and *Hod* is to serve as the sources of prophecy. *Netsah* and *Hod* are represented by the willow branches that are carried on the Feast of Sukkot (Tabernacles).

"Moses is the single human to rise to the level of *Tiferet*, to become 'bridegroom of the *Shekhinah*.'"

The ninth *sefirah* is *Yesod* (Foundation) and represents the joining together of all the cosmic forces. The flow of all the energies above is united once again in a single place; ergo the ninth is parallel to the second *Hokhmah* that began the flow of these forces from a single point. When gathered in *Yesod*, the life animating the *sefirot*, often described in metaphors as light or water, is chiefly notable as male sexual energy, specifically as semen. "The *Sefirotic* process leads to the great union of the nine *sefirot* above, through *Yesod*, with the female *Shekhinah*. She becomes filled and impregnated with the fullness of divine energy and She in turn gives birth to the lower worlds, including both angelic beings and human souls."

Joseph a *tsaddiq* or righteous (a term associated with the ninth *sefira* as G-d is represented as the embodiment of moral righteousness) is the persona associated with *Yesod* since he rejected the wiles of Potiphar's wife, making him a symbol of male chastity or sexual purity. *Yesod* is also designated as *berit* or covenant, again referring to sexual purity through the covenant of circumcision. The ninth *sefira* also stands for male potency as well as sexual purity.

The tenth *sefira* is *Malkhut* (Kingdom) representing the realm over which the King (*Tiferet*) has dominion. As a true king takes responsibility for his kingdom, the King of the universe sustains and protects her. *Malkhut* is the lower world's ruler associated with David the symbol of kingship ever crying out in longing for the blessings of G-d to flow from above (Psalms). While *Malkhut* receives the flow of all the upper *sefirot from Yesod*, She has special affinity for the left side . . . 'the gentle aspect of judgment' but she can also show ruthless vengeance in punishing the wicked. The great drama of religious life is that of protecting *Shekhinah* from the forces of evil and joining Her to the holy Bridegroom who ever awaits Her.

The tenth *sefira* is also referred to as *Shekhinah*.

> She is the moon, dark on her own but receiving and giving off the light of the sun. She is the sea, into whom all waters flow; the earth, longing to be fructified by the rain that falls from heaven. She is the heavenly Jerusalem, into whom the King will enter; She is the throne upon which He is seated, the Temple or Tabernacle, dwelling place of His glory. She is also *Keneset Yisra'el*, the embodied 'Community (or: Assembly) of Israel' itself, identified with the

Jewish people. The tenth *sefira* is a passive/receptive female with regard to the *sefirot* above Her, receiving their energies and being fulfilled by their presence within Her. But She is ruler, source of life, and font of all blessing for the worlds below, including the human soul . . . The separation of *Shekhinah* from the forces above was the terrible sin of Adam that brought about exile from Eden. Yet it is only through Her that humans have access to the mysteries beyond. All prayer is channeled through Her, seeking to energize Her and raise Her up in order to effect the *sefirotic* unity. The primary function of the religious life, with all its duties and obligations, is to rouse the *Shekhinah* into a state of love."[4]

"The *Shekhinah* is called 'the Tree of Knowledge of Good and Evil,' since both Mercy and Power are active in her. When Judgment is in the ascendant, because of sin, the husks, which are the powers of evil, take hold of her, and are nurtured by her. But discussions of Torah encourage the growth of 'the good side' in the *Shekhinah*, and with the help of the good that is in them she becomes united with her Master."[5]

This view of an all-embracing immanence seems to destroy the division between the divine '*sefirot* of emanation' and the lower regions. The latter are arranged in the form of three worlds (creation, formation, and making—*beriyah, yezirah, asiyah*), each of which contains ten *sefirot* or forces. Consequently, the need arose to fix distinct boundaries between these different systems. In the main passage dealing with this problem we read: 'In the ten *sefirot* of emanation the King is there; He and His essence are One there; He and His life are One there. This is not the case with the ten *sefirot* of *beriyah*, for they and their life are not one; they and their essence are not one. And the supreme Cause of all illumines the ten *sefirot* of emanation and the ten (*sefirot*) *of beriyah*, and illumines the ten companies of angels (*yezirah*) and the ten spheres of the firmament *(asiyah)*, and He does not change in any place. The Divine essence is equally present in all realms, but the attachment of the essence to the garments varies according to their nature and status. In the world of emanation a unity exists between the essence and the *sefirot*, while in the other worlds they are in a state of separation. In a description quoted in the continuation of this passage, a different image is used for this distinction: 'In the *sefirot* of emanation there is the actual likeness of the King; in the *sefirot of beriyah*, the seal of the King; in the *sefirot of yezirah*, and among the angels, who are the *Hayyot* (creatures), an impression of the seal in wax.' Immanent divinity is reflected in all worlds, but the degree of brightness or opacity of the mirrors determines the nature of the image. This means that fundamentally, when all is said, and done, the distinction between the world of emanation and the other worlds is simply one of degree, for by nature the *sefirot* of emanation are also distinguished from G-d, while, on the other hand, the self-extending Divine essence dwells, without alteration, even among the lower regions.[6]

The *sefirot* are the divine master-copy of non-divine existence, both in general and in particular. All the worlds and all the beings within and especially humans, are constructed on the pattern of the *sefirot*, 'according to the form that is above.' *Hashem* made the lower world on the same pattern as the upper world, complementing each other, forming a single unity in one whole. All that exists above has its counterpart below. Contemplation of the created world leads to the revelation of the Divine model that is reflected there. The locked gates of the world of emanation can be opened for man to pass through. Knowing the structure of the soul through a grasp of the *sefirot* will provide a connection to the perception of a model and a grasp of the mystery: "When you examine the levels you will find the mystery of wisdom in this matter (i.e., in the structure of the different parts of the soul), and everything is wisdom, that you might perceive in this way matters that are sealed."[7]

Sexual symbolism portrays the life of the Divine in male-female relationship. The sexual terms symbolize how Divine energy flows and are received in the world of emanation. The king *Binah* is supernal king . . . it is female in relation to the supernal point *Hokhmah*, which is concealed from all. Even though it is female it is male in relation to the lower king *Tiferet*. *Yesod* symbolizing the penis reflects ancient phallus worship. The *sefirot* are also symbolic of personalities. Abraham, Isaac and Jacob represent *Hesed, Gevurah,* and *Tiferet*. Moses and Aaron represent *Nezah* and *Hod*. Joseph represents *Yesod*, and David *Malkhut*. *Malkhut* also represents Rachel, Miriam, and Esther. The only one of the three upper *sefirot* symbolized by personality is *Binah* sometimes symbolized by Leah. Abraham showed loving-kindness. Isaac showed fear and his love of Esau is the close relationship that exists in the aspect of judgment (*Din*). *Din* is *Gevurah* and the other side. Jacob is called the perfect man bringing together the two forces of love and judgment in *Tiferet*. *Nezah* and *Hod* appear as twins and serve together as the source of prophecy.

Joseph as the preserver of chastity is *Yesod* which is the sign of the covenant in the realms above (circumcision). King David represents sovereignty . . . according to the *aggadah* his life was not his own; he took some years from the life of Adam; in the same way *Malkhut* has no light of its own but takes its light from *Tiferet*.⁸

> There are a large number of symbols that specifically depict this unstable quality in the nature of the *sefirah*. It is called *shoshanah* (lily) because she changes (*ishtaniat*) from color to color, and varies (*shaniat*) her colors: before intercourse she is green like a rose whose leaves are green and after intercourse she is red with white colors. The *Tiferet* is symbolized by the unchanging white flame of the lamp. *Malkhut* is represented by the lower part of the flame, which is constantly changing colors . . . blue, black and red. This blue-black light sometimes changes to red, but the white light above it never changes for it is always white. *Tiferet* the Tree of Life never changes or turns but *Malkhut* is represented by the Tree of Knowledge of Good and Evil which changes from color to color, from good to evil, and from evil to good . . . and it is consequently called 'the sword that turns,' that turns from one side to the

other, from good to evil, from Mercy to Judgment, from peace to war; it turns through everything.⁹

Primordial man (*Adam Kadmon*) is the symbol of *Yesod*. The righteous (i.e., *Yesod*) take all and posses everything together, and all blessings are contained within him. Adam through his head discharges blessings down like the river flowing out of the Eden. Whenever below enjoys pleasure and delight from the head, and when because of this pleasure and delight they all discharge into him, then he becomes a flowing river going out of real Eden. *Yesod* and *Malkhut* represent male and female which are both channel and storehouse of the Divine powers; they constitute one entity like the unity of the source and the well. This unity is destroyed during exile, when the female is taken away from the male, as a result of the sins of the world. In exile the direction of the world is impaired, because the channel of influence is sealed and the dynamic forces cannot act in the lower realms. Only remnants of the influence, which had previously been sown in the garden of the *Shekhinah*, exist in order to sustain the world. If not for these remnants the world would turn into chaos, for it is the flow of the Divine forces that basically controls and sustains the world.

The fundamental dynamic that keeps the world controlled, directed, and maintained is the continual tension and the balancing of opposites. All of existence is subject to this extreme tension of direct opposites: the leniency of love or mercy with the harshness of judgment; virtues and vices; good and evil; G-d on the other side; the forces of construction and forces of destruction.[10]

In 1918 mathematician Amalie Noether proved an important theorem that shows each fundamental symmetry corresponds to a conservation law of nature. A conservation law states that any physical quantity (energy, momentum, angular momentum, and others) is neither created nor destroyed by interactions, but is transferred in such a way that its total value stays the same. This is not a mysterious arbitrary law but one where the conservation of momentum is the consequence of the fact that the symmetry of an object (e.g., a snowflake) is preserved under sideways translation. In the natural world the fundamental role of symmetry encourages scientists to think that the four forces really are aspects of a single force, and that a theory of everything will be possible to formulate someday. As one might expect from the intimate interrelatedness of particles and forces, the symmetries of the particles are an ingredient of the symmetries of the forces.

Likewise the *sefirot* can be grouped together in symmetrical categories in very much the same way as the physical particles and forces. Primary kabbalistic texts devote extensive efforts to describing the multifold symmetries of the *sefirot*, and then relating these symmetries to other aspects of the Divine system or to the natural world (although written differently). Three kinds of pseudo-symmetries are manifest in the *sefirot:* Two are fundamental and relatively easy to understand: a sexual symmetry of male and female, and geometrical symmetries in which the *sefirot* are described as being either in a linear or spherically concentric relationship. The linear spatial symmetry is echoed in the depiction of the Tree of Life, or in a ladder-like talisman of the *sefirot* in which the left and right sides of the pattern have complementary symmetrical properties.

> The third pseudo-symmetry comes from an association of the *sefirot* with the letters of the Hebrew alphabet, the vowel marks, and the marks that are used for punctuation, decoration, and musical notation for the Torah. These symbols are in turn aligned with symmetries of the human body. Since symmetries lend themselves to a mathematical description, the kabbalistic explorations even sometimes slip into a pseudo-mathematical framework. Words are explored and extensively manipulated both individually and in combinations and permutations that reflect aspects of the *sefirot*.

The symbols are sometimes rotated, rearranged, and combined to illustrate how they can transform into one another. Hebrew letters are also assigned numeric values (*gematria*), so that apparently unrelated words (and therefore concepts) become associated by their mathematic equivalences or other mathematic relationships. G-d's ineffable four-letter name is also explicated with numerous substitutions and inversions, some of which build on principles of symmetry. In the kabbalah, many symmetries follow as a natural result of the dialectical pairing of *sefirot*, while the qualities of symmetry itself can be thought of as resulting from the distinctive beauty of *Tiferet*, the sixth of the *sefirot*, whose radiance results from the convergence of the open plenitude of *Hesed* (the fourth *sefirah*) with the constraining regularities of *Gevurah* (the fifth *sefirah*).[11]

The *sefirot* are continuous channels of Divine influence to the universe and not just processes active only in the earliest moments of the Creation. *Gevurah* was not only the dominant *sefirah* functioning during the epoch of leptons, but also the straining and shaping the uniformly expanding material into galaxies and stars. As the evolving world took form the great pressures produced by constriction and separation led inevitably to the introduction of negativity into the universe, the result of what is termed the 'breaking of the vessels,' the 'containers' for the light of the *sefirot*. The rupturing of these metaphoric vessels represents the world's imperfection.[12]

> The explanation of creation in the language of modern physics helps to clarify the kabalah's imagery of the Creation. The living G-d Who is Blessed created the universe and life from principles of gravity, a manifestation of Divine love. Divine love (*ahavah*) is subsumed in *Keter*, the highest of the *sefirot*, the source of self-attraction and gravity. It is withheld by *Hokhmah* until the 'spontaneous symmetry breaking' of the strong force releases energy into the inflation during the *sefirah* of *Binah*. This freed energy of attraction then cools and condenses during the phases of *Hesed* and *Gevurah*, generating the first stable particles of matter and initiating our new world. The kabbalah of course does not put things this way, but it does use metaphors of attraction followed by phased expansion that lend themselves to this physical interpretation. And why was the world created at all? Arguments from the

strong anthropic principle and quantum mechanics suggest one answer: the purpose of the existence of the universe is intelligent life, whose free will and awareness ground the universe.[13]

Jacob attained the rung of *Tif'eret* and was able to marry two sisters (Leah and Rachel), who respectively symbolized *Binah* and *Shekhinah*. His marriage in the world below stimulated the union of *Tif'eret* with both females in the world above. However, anyone other than Jacob who marries two sisters impairs the *sefirotic* process, disrupting the union of the divine females and turning them against one another. The wording "expose nakedness above and below . . ." apparently applies to *Binah* (above) and *Shekhinah* (below), but may also imply the *sefirotic* world above and the human family below.[13]

> The first letter of the YHVH resembles a point and signifies the primordial point of *Hokhmah,* which emerged from the hidden unknowable realm of *Keter* and *Ein Sof.* This radiant point comprises the totality of all *sefirotic* lights. When it was stimulated by the hidden source, the subtle radiant point of *Hokhmah* generated the blissful radiance of *Binah,* which it then entered in rapture, hiding itself away.

Within the radiant bliss of *Binah* were fashioned the designs of six *sefirot* from *Hesed* through *Yesod*, known only to the subtle light of *Hokhmah* uniting with *Binah*. The radiance of *Binah*, issuing from *Hokhmah*, contains the roots of Judgment and is thus described as fearsome and awesome. As the six *sefirot* within Her gestated and grew numerous, Her womb expanded. When she gave birth to them, they constituted a complete totality of six, symbolized by the letter *vav*, whose numerical value is six. This letter joined with the concealed world of *Hokhmah* and *Binah*, symbolized by the letters *yod* and *he*, the components of the name *Yah*. Together, all three letters constitute the name *YHV*.[14]

The conclusion of the verse in Psalms for Jacob has chosen *Yah* for himself describes all of Jacob's descendants: Israel, to his own treasure, impling that no other Israelite is permitted to ascend to the attained heights of Jacob. Israelites strive to reach the realm of *Shekhinah*, the divine treasure filled with the riches of emanation. From within the realm of *Shekhinah* they may draw on higher *sefirot* through contemplation (secrecy of aspiration). They may not openly draw on higher *sefirot* openly as did Jacob.

In the second verse of the Torah portion Rabbi Shim'on gives an interpretation of "Speak to the Children of Israel and have them take Me (*terumah*), an offering." (Exodus 25:2) The word *terumah* derives from the root *rum* to rise, and can be rendered: raised contribution, offering, donation, gift. He interprets the word hyperliterally as raising or rising alluding to contemplative ascent, or to *Shekhinah*, who rises through prayer to unite with *Tif'eret*. The verse now implies: Have them take Me (i.e., they may attain My higher realms by rising contemplative prayer, or by raising *Shekhinah*, who is known as rising).[14]

In the Garden of *Shekhinah* the primordial light is hidden, or sown, by *Yesod*, yielding fruit to nourish the world every day. *Yesod* conveys creative power to *Shekhinah* and fashions the lower worlds and generates all souls. Heaven and earth symbolize the Divine couple alluded to in the opening verse of Genesis. Their mysterious union engendered the *mishkan* (Dwelling, Tabernacle), which thus reflects the structure of the *sefirot* and of the entire cosmos. G-d instructs Moses in Exodus, to ask the Israelites to donate materials to construct the Dwelling, and the phrase *li terumah* (Me an offering), alludes to *Yesod* or *Tif'eret* (Me), and *Shekhinah* (an offering), "joined as one."[15]

The primordial light of the first day of Creation symbolizes *Hesed*. This light entered the pavilion *of Shekhinah* by means of *Yesod* (Foundation), impregnating Her, and *Shekhinah* produced an image of the light. The verse reads "And there was light," rather than 'And it was so,' as with nearly all the other commands of Creation. Rabbi Shim'on explains that the repetition of the word light indicates that this light resembled the primordial light.

The division of waters on the second day of Creation symbolizes the division within *Shekhinah* between the flow of *Hesed* on the right and that of *Gevurah* on the left. This division was made by a fiery flow from *Gevurah*. Then *Shekhinah* produced an image of the dividing force, which became the firmament described in Genesis.[16]

One of the revealed mysteries of the Torah is that certain letters are written large while others are written small. "The entire small alphabet in many cases is associated with Shekhinah (lower world) and the large alphabet with Binah (upper world, also known as the World that is Coming)."[17]

The Torah symbolizes *Tif'eret* that emanates from *Hokhmah* (wisdom); it is known as Primordial Torah and *qodesh*, Holiness. *Hokhmah* emanates from the highest *sefirah*, *Keter*, known as Holy of Holies.

Keter represents *Ayin* (Nothingness) or the Divine no-thingness. *Keter* is the undifferentiated and incomprehensible essence of G-d. The verse in Job reads as a rhetorical question: "Wisdom, *me-ayin*, whence, does she come?" Mystically the verse yields a description of the first two *sefirot*; Wisdom comes *me-ayin*, from nothingness.

Jubilee symbolizes *Binah*, the Divine Mother who is married to *Hokhmah* and who shares His name, Holiness (as indicated in the verse from Leviticus). *Tif'eret* is symbolized by Israel, whose full name is *Tif'eret Yisra'el* (Beauty of Israel). *Tif'eret's* parents, *Hokhmah*, and *Binah* reflects the qualities of Israel and are both called Holiness. Since Israel is composed of both these divine parents, the people of Israel are called people of holiness.[18]

> In Song of Songs, the maiden compares her beloved to an apple tree. The Midrash interprets the entire biblical book as a love song between the Assembly of Israel and her Divine beloved. From a kabbalistic

perspective, Assembly of Israel signifies not only the people of Isreal but also their divine counterpart, *Shekhinah*, who sings to *Tif'eret*, the blessed Holy One. *Tif'eret* is like an apple because He combines the respective colors of *Hesed, Gevurah,* and *Tif'eret*: white, red, and green, corresponding to the white of the apple's pulp, the red of the skin, and the green of the leaves.

The various laws contained in this Torah portion, *Mishpatim* (Laws) follows the account of the revelation on Mount Sinai. Rabbi Yose explains that the Torah was given from the side of *Gevurah* (Power) on the left. To balance the severity of this *sefirah*, G-d sought to ensure peace and harmony among Israel by giving them laws of justice. Thereby, Torah would manifest both the strictness of *Gevurah* and the grace of *Hesed,* and the world would endure through balanced Justice.[19]

Sin ruins the harmony above, splitting the divine couple and interrupting the flow of blessing. *Tif'eret* (symbolized by compassion) separates from *Shekhinah,* and She no longer conveys emanation to those below. So G-d obliterates human transgression for My own sake to ensure that *Shekhinah* will continue to receive the flow. The wandering Jew is playing on *le-ma'ani* (for My own sake), and *yitman'un* (will be withheld).[20]

Humans were created in the image of G-d and therefore the human body resembles the sefirotic body. There are three aspects of the soul: *nefesh* (soul, animating the human being), *ruah* (spirit, breath), and *neshamah* (breath, soul). Each of the three aspects derives from its own sefirotic source: *Shekhinah, Tiferet,* and *Binah*. The three aspects of the soul are united just as the sefirot are united. Virtuous acts enhance all three aspects, whereas evil acts defile all three aspects.[21] "Everyone is born with *nefesh*, but *ruah* and *neshamah* must be achieved. Yet even someone who has attained all three aspects of soul must strive to maintain their purity. How can one determine if a person has reached this advanced state? Can s/he control his/her temper. If someone is overwhelmed by anger, in effect s/he has uprooted his/her *neshamah* (the holiest aspect of soul) and supplanted it with an alien god, a wrathful spirit."[22]

"The name *Yah* alludes to *Hokhman* and *Binah,* parents of the lower *sefirot*, since *yod* symbolizes *Hokhmah* and *he* symbolizes *Binah*; so the twelve boundaries are called tribes of

Yah. The full name of *Tiferet*, the core of the boundaries, is *Tiferet Yisra'el*, so *Yah* is called a testimony to Israel."[23]

In Rabbinic tradition G-d created other worlds and destroyed them . . . eventually *Ein Sof* emanated the *sefirot* through which He fashioned this world. At Creation everything that was at His presence was prefigured in the sefirot and came to exist. "That which is has already been . . . and what is to be already has been." The creation of the world is not entirely new, either because earlier creations preceded it or because G-d recycled the remains of those earlier worlds into this world.[24]

The Zohar's commentary on Leviticus deals largely with the spiritualization of the laws and procedures dealing with animal offerings, grain offerings, and priestly ritual that are transformed into symbols of G-d's inner life. The ascent offerings that were totally consumed on the altar are called *olah* (that which ascends) and symbolize *Shekhinah*, last of the ten *sefirot* who ascends to unite with Her beloved, the blessed Holy One.[25]

Tiferet (blessed Holy One) enters the heavenly Garden of Eden to unite with the Assembly of Israel (*Shekhinah*). The day the Dwelling was built not only did the holy couple unite but all six lower *sefirot (Hesed* through *Yesod)* united with one another. They were watered by the stream issuing from *Binah*. All the worlds below (the angels and the lower worlds) were also nourished. The offering of the aroma below stimulates the flow of blessing above.[26]

The name YHVH symbolizes all of the *sefirot* which function harmoniously, with paths diverging to the right (*Hesed*) and to the left (*Gevurah* or *Din*).[27] The first letter *yod* in YHVH has a traditional shape that includes a tip at the top left, a tip at the bottom, and the body of the letter. The tip above symbolizes *Keter* (Crown), the first *sefirah*.[28] The main body of the letter *yod* symbolizes *Hokhmah,* the primordial point, which is the origin of all the lower *sefirot* and more concealed than all of them. The name YHVH is based on the initial letter.[29] The bottom tip of *yod* is symbolized by *Binah* which issues the flow of emanation watering *Shekhinah* (symbolized by the Garden) and the *sefirot* from *Hesed* through *Yesod* (pictured as plants).[30]

PROPHETS

The prophet Ezekiel in a vision saw four creatures, each of whom had four faces: the face of a human being in front, the face of a lion on the right, the face of an ox on the left, and the face of an eagle at the back. (Ezekiel 1:10) Here the demonic officials Afrira and Kastimon resemble the creatures who appear on the left and the back before combining into a human image.[1] Israel's vision of G-d surpassed even that of Ezekiel, who saw the divine chariot-throne whirling through the heavens.

> He opened seven compartments down below. Ezekiel gazed into these in order to see all that is on high. These are the seven compartments down below: *Adamah* (Ground); *Erez* (Earth); *Heled* (World); *Nehsiyyah* (Forgetfulness); *Dumah* (Silence); *She'ol* (Pit); and *Tit ha-Yaven* (Miry Clay). Where is *Adamah* mentioned? In the verse: 'The ground did cleave.' (Numbers 16:31) Where is *Erez* mentioned?

In the verse: 'And the earth opened her mouth.' (Numbers 16:32) Where is the *Heled* mentioned? In the verse: 'Give ear all ye inhabitants of the world.' (Psalms 49:2) Where is the *Nehsiyyah* mentioned? In the verse: 'And Thy righteousness in the land of forgetfulness.' (Psalms 88:13) Where is the *Dumah* mentioned? In the verse: 'Neither any that go down into silence.' (Psalms 115:7) Where is the *She'ol* mentioned? In the verse: 'So they, and all that appertained to them went down alive into the pit.' (Numbers 16:33) Where is the *Tit ha-Yaven* mentioned? In the verse: 'He brought me up also out of the tumultuous pit, and out of the miry clay.' (Psalms 40:2)[2]

As a result of Israel's lack of faith and their insolence, not only was Amalek empowered on earth, but above in the *sefirotic* realm harsh Judgment nearly overwhelmed Compassion . . . the quality of *Tiferet Yisra'el* (Beauty of Israel), namely Israel above. Moses who attained the rung of *Tiferet,* had to focus on this battle. The battle of Amalek was a cosmic battle, more fateful than any other in the history of the world, because the Divine realm itself was affected . . . both by the *sefirotic* struggle and by Amalek's violent mockery of heaven. The concept of Gog and Magog as demonic powers who will wage eschatological war against the righteous and be defeated by G-d is from Ezekiel 38:2.[3]

"Transgressors of Israel who sin with their body and transgressors of the Gentiles who sin with their body descend to Hell and are punished there for twelve months. After twelve months, their body is consumed, their soul burned, and the wind scatters them under the soles of the feet of the righteous . . . But as for heretics, informers, apostates, skeptics, those who rejected Torah and denied the resurrection of the dead, those who abandoned the ways of the community, those who spread their terror in the land of the living (Ezekiel 32:23), and those who sinned and made the masses sin . . . : these descend to Hell and are punished there for generation after generation . . . Hell will be consumed, but they will not be consumed." (BT Rosh ha Shanah 17a)

"In the days of Ezra and Nehemiah, the leaders of the Israelites prayed that the evil impulse be eliminated. The impulse to commit idolatry was handed over to them, and they cast it into a lead pot with a lead cover, rendering it powerless. They prayed further and the sexual impulse was also handed over to them, but a prophet warned, 'Realize that if you kill him, the world will be destroyed (because the desire to procreate will vanish).' They imprisoned him for three days, and looked in the whole land of Israel for a fresh egg and could not find it. They said, 'What should we do? If we kill him, the world will be destroyed.' . . . They blinded him and let him go. This helped inasmuch as he no longer entices a person to commit incest." BT Yoma 69b

"Here the lead pot is replaced by 'an iron signet ring in the hollow of the great abyss.' This hollow is the demonic dwelling. Once the evil impulse reappeared, passions were aroused again and the fire of Hell was rekindled." "Hell has seven entrances and the wicked are assigned to one of the seven habitations of Hell, corresponding to their sinfulness."[4]

> The Book of Adam . . . contains the genealogy of the entire human race. Rabbi Shim'on discovered there a description of Elijah, whose spirit descended to earth and was clothed in a human body until he ascended to heaven in the whirlwind. At this point, his body remained suspended in the whirlwind, while his spirit donned a body of light, in which Elijah entered the company of the angels. Whenever necessary Elijah descends again, clothing himself in the body preserved in the whirlwind, in order to carry out divine missions in the world. In Jewish tradition Elijah is associated with the Messianic age.[5]

DEMONS, DEVILS, SATAN, EVIL

The second day of Creation symbolizes the second of the seven lower *sefirot*, *Gevurah*, or *Din* (Judgment), on the left. The quality of Judgment conflicts with *Hesed*, and this division is reflected by the creation of the firmament on the second day, dividing the upper waters from the lower waters. Hell, an extreme manifestation of harsh Judgment also emerges on the second day; it is pictured as the dross of the fiery left side.[1]

Rabbi El'azar offers a cryptic, veiled description of the origin of evil, whose ultimate source is the holy right side. Apparently, the thirteen springs issue from the highest realms of divinity and generate a thousand streams . . . and thirteen other streams, which gather water from nine hundred and ninety-nine of the thousand. The two remaining halves of the thousandth stream rejoin, and the resulting single stream enters the thirteen 'other' streams, becoming a demonic serpent.[2]

Two fallen angels (Uzza and Aza'el) opposed the creation of Adam and Eve and fell from heaven. They were attracted by the daughters of humankind, and inherited dust. These two angels are identified with the two spies sent by Joshua to Jericho, apparently based on the image of angels spying on human beings. The human daughters are seen as demonic figures and identified with the two prostitutes who approached King Solomon, each claiming to be the mother of the same infant. Solomon's wisdom enabled him to overwhelm these demonic forces that previously could not be vanquished.[3] Genesis 6:2 discusses Uzza and Azael who were attracted by the daughters of men and punished by being bound in chains of iron in the mountains of darkness, from where they still manage to wreak havoc, teaching sorcery to humans.[4]

During the time of Ezra and Nehemiah Israel's leaders were handed the impulse to commit idolatry and they cast it in a lead pot with a lead cover rendering it powerless. With additional prayer the sexual impulse was also handed over to them and after being warned about its importance to procreation it was blinded and freed instead of being destroyed. "The lead pot was replaced by 'an iron signet ring in the hollow of the great abyss.' This hollow is the demonic dwelling. Once the evil impulse reappeared, passions were aroused again and the fire of Hell was rekindled."[5] During sexual union, if one is dominated by the lust of the evil impulse, then the body formed through that act will be tainted. The soul will be compelled to inhabit (or become married to) such an alien body and will be unable to manifest holiness in the world. Upon leaving the body (or this world), such a soul will not partake of spiritual sustenance and bliss (the sacred donations).[6] In time of calamity, one should not go outside, exposing himself to destructive forces. (Exodus 12:22) Once permission has been granted to the Destroyer, he does not distinguish between the righteous and the wicked. One should not walk in the middle of the road because the Angel of Death walks there, for as soon as permission has been granted to him, he strides brazenly.[7]

As darkness falls, the demonic powers demand the ways of the house of the King so as to seek to know what has been decreed above, so that they can execute judgment on earth. Sleep (BT Berakhot 57b) is one-sixtieth of death. At night when the impure powers have descended to earth, the angels are unimpeded and can rise higher to praise G-d through the three watches of the night. By descending to earth and casting sleep (a taste of death) upon the world the angels relegate the demonic (deathly) force to rule humanity. This frees the angels to approach G-d directly and praise Him.[8]

"The world is maintained through a rhythm of light and darkness, good and evil. Human choice and action determine which power will manifest on earth: the divine or the demonic. The demonic forces, too, serve a sacred function by punishing human evil."[9] Hell has seven entrances and the wicked are assigned to one of the seven habitations of Hell, corresponding to their sinfulness.[10]

Deuteronomy commands against plowing with an ox and donkey which symbolize demonic powers and is a warning not to stimulate the union of the two dangerous forces. The two demonic forces on the left (ox) and right (donkey) generate an even more impudent one, known as dog. Amalek's impudence derives from the demonic dog. In Exodus 11 during the tenth plague the Israelites were not even menaced by a dog. "No dog will sharpen its tongue (i.e., threaten or snarl). Joshua 10:21[11]

Rabbi Abba compares existence to a nut with various layers; a thin outer sheath, a hard shell within, a thin shell further within, and finally the kernel. These correspond, respectively, to the physical world, the demonic hard shell (ruling the body), a thin shell, and the holy kernel.[12] The demonic "other side" has no power over the Holy Land, where its shell is split wide open and blessing pervades the land. As long as Israel brought offerings in the Temple, this opening endured and holiness prevailed. However, when the people sinned, this stimulated the demonic shell to close the opening, obstructing holiness and dooming the Temple to destruction and the people to exile.[13] The thin covering protecting the Holy Land derives from a higher curtain that protects the holy realm above from demonic forces. When a Gentile dwelling in the Holy Land dies, his soul is not accepted by this covering nor allowed to ascend through it, and such souls are forced to roam until finally reaching the realm of impurity. When a Jew dies in the Holy Land, his soul is welcomed by the thin covering and conveyed to holiness above.[14]

With the *sefirot* of "the other side" each *sefirah* is stamped with the seal of individuality. The Zohar describes the personal characteristics of Samael and Lilith, the male and female who comprise and reflect the whole system of the husks. Samael is counted among the angels as the head angel of destruction . . . he is the guardian angel of Esau-Edom. Lilith is portrayed as an evil spirit with human characteristics. Before Eve Lilith attempted intercourse with Adam and one version has her becoming pregnant by Adam. Once Eve arrived, Lilith fled and plotted to kill babies ever since. She dwells in the cities of the sea and in the days to come G-d will have her dwell in the ruins of Rome. She rears demons born as the result of intercourse with evil spirits and humans. Lilith becomes the tenth *sefirah* of the other side like the *Shekhinah* in the *sefirot* of holiness.[15]

Naamah came from Tubal-cain and helps Lilith. Humans go astray after her. She flames desire in men's dreams and conceives by those who lust after her and bears demons. These demons seduce mortal women and Naamah joins Lilith in killing little children. Our souls leave us at night during sleep and ascend on high. The soul goes through many levels and is confronted by the deceiving lights of uncleanness. If it is pure and was not defiled during the day it ascends to higher realms. If it is not pure it joins the uncleanness and does not rise further. The secret of dreams is that the pure soul receives truth about things and the future while the soiled soul is given misleading untrue information.

Erev Rav means mixed multitude and refers to "sons of Lilith" i.e., their souls cleave to the other side. They first entered the world through Cain as a result of intercourse between Eve and the serpent. So *erev rav* in every generation are descended from Cain and their souls' source is the Tree of Knowledge of Good and Evil since it was through eating its fruit that Adam and Eve lost their purity by being infected with pollution from the serpent. *Erev rav* souls are a mixture of good and evil. It was the souls possessed by the wicked in the generation of the flood and whose survivors built the Tower of Babel in the generation of dispersion. Moses' soul originated with Abel and he wanted to blot out the record of the first murder by reforming the children of Cain.

The Zohar indicates Cain was formed from both Adam's seed and the serpent's slime. The fallen angel Samael is identified with the serpent. The spirits and demons associated with Cain are half human and half angelic. Cain inherited traits of the upper world; from Adam he inherited traits of the lower world.[16]

Five types of *erev rav*:

1. *Amalekim*—Balaam and Balak were from the side of Amalek . . . those that survived in the fourth exile were oppressive leaders that opposed Israel with weapons of violence.
2. *Nefilim*—are from the world above and are cast down in order to lust for beautiful women.
3. *Gibborim*—they build and do not for *Hashem* but to make a name for themselves. They build cities, synagogues, schools, etc. and get strength from *sitra otra*.
4. *Rephaim*—they forsake Israel in bitter straits for they have the power to save but not the desire. They forsake

the Torah and those who study it, in order to deal kindly with idolaters.
5. *Anakim*—they despise those of whom it is said 'They shall be necklaces (*anakim*) about your neck.'[17]

The heel symbolizes the demonic, lowest realm, linked with Esau. Jacob's name means 'He grips the heel,' trying to prevent the prior birth of his twin. The Zohar implies that Jacob grips the heel in order to subdue evil. The heels are demonic forces who spy on carefree sinners.[18]

You shall not boil a kid in its mother's milk. According to Rabbi Abba, a kid symbolizes the demonic power, while mother refers to *Shekhinah* (Assembly of Israel), who nurtures the world. These two elements must not be mingled, lest the demonic force imbibe the rich flow of the Mother. The sequence of these two verses implies that if the people of Israel violate the divine command and mingle the demonic kid with the divine mother, then G-d will separate Himself from them and only an angel will accompany them.[19]

The phrase 'impure woman' refers to a menstruant or the demonic female who lusts for divine potency, imploring the divine male to lie beside her. The erotic tone is highlighted by the fact that Joseph symbolizes specifically the *sefirah* of *Yesod*, the divine phallus. Normally, *Yesod* channels all divine energy to *Shekhinah*; but as a result of human sinfulness (such as being seduced by a foreign woman), the demonic female can supplant *Shekhinah*, receive the potency of *Yesod* herself, and tyrannize the world.[20]

Midrashic tradition says that when Babylonian envoys came to visit King Hezekiah, he showed them not only his own treasures but also the treasure of the Holy of Holies and the two tablets of the covenant within the ark. By exposing the holiest treasures of the Temple, Hezikiah rendered it vulnerable both to demonic forces above and to the Babylonians on earth.[21]

> The dust is the serpent, the power of uncleanness, which ruled over the land of Israel at the time of the Temple's destruction. It also ruled there earlier, before Israel had conquered the land, and is called 'the Canaanite,' mentioned in the verse quoted. Genesis 12:6[22]

> The phrase (*mi-qets yamim*) is usually taken to mean "in the course of time," but here Rabbi Shim'on focuses on the literal meaning: "at the end of days," which he understands as referring to the demonic

power that appears as the Angel of Death, bringing an end to the days of every mortal creature. Cain's offering was not accepted because it derived from (or was intended for) the demonic realm, not from (or for) *Shekinhah,* who is known as *(qets yamin)*, 'the end of the right'—the consummation of the divine flow, characterized by the grace of the right side. Cain rejected *Shekhinah* in favor of the demonic power.[23]

Cain is referred to as the 'son of slime' since he was born from the union of the serpent and Eve. The serpent-rider (Samael) copulated with her and she conceived Cain. Afterward Adam copulated with her and she conceived Abel. Even Abel was not fully refined, since he was still tainted by the demonic. Seth, the third child of Adam and Eve, generated the righteous.[24]

The view of Cain is as the progenitor of demons that were cruel and brazen as Cain was the product of a union between the serpent and Eve. Abel procreated some demons as well; they were far gentler and at times could be some benefit to mankind. Adam's semen was mixed with the 'filth' of the serpent to produce Abel so his demons were not as cruel as those from Cain. When Adam separated from Eve after the death of Abel, he had intercourse with spirits and produced demons that were half angels and half men. The spirits and the demons are half like humans below and half like angels above. The evil inclination is a Jewish demon . . . this demon is like Moses' rod, which changed from a rod to a snake, and then from a snake to a rod. Likewise the demon changes from a demon to an angel and from an angel to a demon depending on man's deeds.

. . . If a soul (G-d's daughter) passes through the cosmic scales when sins abound in the world, the scales tip toward impurity and that soul falls into the hands of Lilith, the demonic slave-girl, who torments her. Tormented souls inhabit the bodies of certain babies, suckling at the breast. G-d foresees that if these infants endure in the world they will degenerate and sin, so He allows Lilith to kill them while they are still pure. In this way man explains the tragic death of babies.[25]

All souls exist individually since Creation. Before descending to earth, each soul is clothed in an ethereal body resembling the physical body she will inhabit on earth; she retains this while in the physical body until shortly before death, and then regains it afterward. Here, the soul worries that it will be subjugated to physical needs and desires, and soiled by the body's submission to the evil impulse.[26]

Some are tormented because in a previous lifetime they tormented others; some suffer because their parents or ancestors sinned, stretching back several generations. Another type of sinner is one who oppresses his fellow. He will be tormented by the suffering of his children at the hands of the demonic power.[27]

In heaven, the tears of babies who have died protect the living. They weep and study in the Heavenly Academy, leaning Torah directly from G-d. The verse in Psalms indicates that from the mouth of babes and sucklings G-d establishes (a heavenly school of) Torah, which is known as strength. Their study of Torah defeats demonic forces that threaten Israel below.[28]

Normally, G-d first fashions the outer layer (or shell) to protect the subsequent inner layer (or kernel). Although the kernel emerges only later, it arises in divine thought first. Whereas the protective shell derives from the demonic realm (the Other Side), the kernel derives from the realm of holiness. Once the kernel (or fruit) has matured, the shell is discarded.

"Righteous One of the world" designates *Yesod*, who channels the divine flow to *Shekhinah* and, through Her, to the worlds below. As for the heavenly Temple that will descend to earth at the time of Redemption, both kernel and shell are divine. Therefore G-d begins with the kernel, building the Temple itself (represented by Zion); then He constructs the shell, the walls of Jerusalem. These walls are constituted by divine fire, not by the 'Other Side.' Just as the kernel precedes the shell in divine thought, so Israel arose in G-d's mind before all other nations. And just as the shell precedes the kernel in formation, so the rulers of Edom reigned before any king reigned over the Children of Israel. However, in the time of Redemption, Israel (the kernel) will precede all other nations (the shell) and be fully protected.[29]

BT *Shabbat* 55b "Four died through the incitement of the serpent, namely: Benjamin the son of Jacob, Amram the father of Moses, Jesse the father of David, and Chileab the son of David." This view states they did not sin on their own but died only because of the sin of Adam and Eve, who were enticed by the serpent.[30]

The selling of Joseph by his ten brothers was eventually punished through the martyrdom of ten rabbis during the Hadrianic persecution in the second century CE. After the brothers sold Joseph permission was granted to Samael to annihilate ten heroes in their place.[31]

When Israel came out of Egypt, the angel Samael arose to accuse them, saying before the blessed Holy One, "Master of the World! Until now, they were worshiping idols, and now You are splitting the sea for them?" What did the blessed Holy One do? He handed over to him Job, who was one of Pharaoh's advisers, of whom is written "a man blameless and upright (Job 1:8); and He said to him, "Here, he is in your hand" (Job 2:6). The blessed Holy One thought, "While he occupies himself with Job, Israel will go through the sea, and afterward I will deliver Job." Job said: "He handed me over to Satan. I order that Israel would not emerge guilty in judgment, He wrung me out through his hand." At that moment, the blessed Holy One said to Moses, "Moses! Look, I have handed Job over to Satan. What should you do? Speak to the Children of Israel and have them journey forward!" (Exodus 14:15)[32]

> By repenting and turning back to G-d, Israel fulfills the purpose of exile and her suffering is completed even before all the intended 'generations' of exile have appeared. Thereby the 'evil extremity' namely the demonic dominion of exile is terminated, along with its control and 'ownership' of Israel and redemption arrives.[33]
>
> The covering of the Dwelling comprised four separate layers: linen, goat hair, ram skins, and,

uppermost, leather. The linen curtains constituting the innermost layer are very holy; covering them are curtains of *izzim,* goat hair suggesting *sa'ir,* goat, demon, satyr, and the scapegoat sent to the demon Azazel (Leviticus 16). These goat-hair curtains symbolize powers outside the divine realm that protect the inner, holy powers.[34]

"According to Rabbi Shim'on, the sorcerers Yannes and Yambres were the sons of Balaam whose father Beor is identical with Laban (Rebekah's brother). They understood *Shekhinah,* the Cup of Blessing, receives the flow of emanation from *Hesed,* on the right side. Being themselves linked to the left side, they approached Aaron (who symbolizes *Hesed*) so that he would invigorate and complete them."[35] "Conversely, the demonic Other Side is bodiless and also has no share in the divine body."[36]

Demons are present at night even in a town, and at all times in places frequented by demonic spirits: ruins, unyielding fields, and desolate wilderness.[37] In the Zohar Dogs are euphemisms for demonic powers. BT Yoma 21b observes that in the First Temple the fire on the altar appeared crouching like a lion, while in the Second Temple it crouched like a dog.[38]

The Zohar mentions that "All attains equilibrium . . ." comes from a verse in Job that questions who can produce pure from Impure? No one can. The Almighty can. Pure issues only from impure . . . namely man can regain purity only when the impure forces are removed.[39] "Even evil originates in the divine realm, having its roots in the *sefirah* of *Gevurah*, or *Din* (Judgment). Human action stimulates action above, as does human speech."[40]

NUMBERS, COLORS, HEBREW LETTERS AND WORDS

The mysterious name YHVH is not pronounced according to its letters, but rather according to the letters of the more revealed name *Adonai*, thereby maintaining the secrecy of the holier name. Similarly, the Torah is revealed in its simple meaning, while its deeper significance is secret. This principle applies universally.[1]

As a book written in code through the use of symbolism, euphemisms, figures of speech, ancient phraseology, and the Hebrew Bible or *Tenakh* the Zohar also utilizes numerology *(gimatriyya)*, colors, and the physical shape of Hebrew letters. The *gimatriyya* provides the serious sojourner with many "ah-ha" moments, as does the symbolism of colors. Utilizing meditations and prayers the mind-heart connection can be enhanced by long and deep concentration on colors and Hebrew letters.

In order to better comprehend the hidden, this chapter is dedicated to numbers, colors, and Hebrew letters and words. The *gimatriyya* of YHVH and Adam have numerical values like all the words in the Torah.²

> According to *gimatryyia* (the system of assigning a numerical value to each Hebrew letter according to its sequence in the alphabet) *tsitsit* has the numerical equivalence of 600 (*tsadi* 90 + *yod* 10 + *tsadi* 90 + *yod* 10 + *tav* 400), plus the 8 strings in each bundle and 5 knots on the bundle total 613, the traditional number of commandments in the Torah. So may I too enwrap my soul—my 248 limbs and 365 sinews (also totaling 613)—in the effulgence of the 613 supernal fringes.³

One desert hermit discovered a deeper meaning of *mevorakh* in a dream. The first two letters *mem* and *bet* are numerically equivalent to forty-two, alluding to the Name of forty-two letters, by which G-d created the world. *Mem* and *bet* signify hardness and harshness, since *Hashem* created the world by Judgment as indicated by the appearance of the name *Elohim* (associated with judgment) in the opening verse of Genesis: "In the beginning *Elohim* created the heaven and the earth." Rosh Hashanah celebrates Creation and is the Day of Judgment characterized by the letters *mem* and *bet*. Rosh Hashanah yields to the softness of *Shemini Atseret* (eighth day of assembly) when G-d rejoices with Israel following the purging of Yom Kippur and the celebration of Sukkot. This softness is represented by the last two letters of *mevorakh*, blessed, which spell the *rakh*, soft.[4]

There are four spices for Sukkot that consist of seven elements. Traditionally there are three sprigs of myrtle and two willow twigs along with the *lulas* and *etrog* totaling four spices, not seven. The three others are the second and third sprigs of myrtle and the second willow twig. By holding all seven elements together and shaking them, we arouse the seven lower *sefirot*, stimulating a flow of blessing.[5]

Forty-nine gates of *Binah* are revealed in four lower *sefirot*, corresponding to the four directions: *Hesed* (south), *Gevurah* (north), *Tif'eret* (east), and *Shekhinah* (west). The fiftieth gate remains hidden: it "has no side and is shut." The word *Be-reshit* contains two words: *bara* (created) referring to the hidden mystery of creation, and *shit* (six) referring to the revelation of the six *sefirot*.[6]

"Once you have enthroned Him above and below and in the four directions of heaven, you need do nothing more."

(*Berakhot* 13b) These six directions (above, below, north, south, east, and west) symbolize the six *sefirot* from *Hesed* through *Yesod*, which join in preparation for the union with *Shekhinah*. The first six words of the *Shema* contain six words in Hebrew . . . by reciting these six with intention one unifies the corresponding six *sefirot*.[7]

According to *Sefer Yetsirah* 1:1-2, G-d created the world by means of 'thirty-two wondrous paths of wisdom,' namely, the twenty-two letters of the Hebrew alphabet and the ten *sefirot*.[8]

The four letters of the word *ahavah* (love) correspond to the letters of YHVH, which signify the four *sefirot Hesed, Gevurah, Tif'eret,* and *Shekhinah*, who constitute a supernal chariot for *Binah*. From the union of the four spirits (symbolized by the four letters), a new spirit is formed, named Love, who ascends to the heavenly Palace of Love, stimulating this palace to unite with a higher realm.[9]

> *Sefer Yetsirah* 2:2, 5 describes the mystery of the twenty-two Hebrew letters: Twenty-two elemental letters. He engraved them, carved them, weighted them, and permuted and combined them, forming with them everything formed and everything destined to be formed . . . Twenty-two elemental

letters. He set them in a wheel with 231 gates, turning forward and backward . . . How did He permute them? *Alef* with them all, all of them with *alef*; *bet* with them all, all of them with *bet*; and so with all the letters turning round and round . . .

These letters began to whirl and combine, initiating the process of creation by the engraving of the Holy Name, which may allude to the combination of each letter of the alphabet with each of the letters YHVH. The letters emerged in reverse order, from *tav* to *alef*, and once the letter *yod* (the first letter of YHVH) completed its creative turn, G-d said, 'enough!' The next letter, *tet*, was stranded in the air above one particular spot on earth, which happened to be right where the man from Luz would some day found his new city. Since *tet* symbolizes life, that location has been immune to the Angel of Death since the world began.

The numerical value of *tet* is nine, which can allude to the ninth *sefirah*, *Yesod*, the divine phallus and river of life. The association of *tet* with life is also linked to the fact that this letter begins the word *tov* (good).[10]

The days of the week correspond to cosmic *sefirotic* days above. Sunday through Friday symbolize respectively *Hesed* through *Yesod*, while Sabbath symbolizes *Binah* and also *Shekhinah*. Each mundane day is blessed by its supernal day, all six of which are blessed by the seventh day, *Binah*. Thus every day conveys a unique blessing to the world, and therefore Moses insisted that each day's portion of manna should be consumed on that particular day. On Friday a double portion appeared for that day and the Sabbath. In Creation each day is named but only the sixth day appears with the definitive article *ha* for 'the' that serves as a feminine marker alluding to *Shekhinah*, symbolized by the final *hay* in YHVH. The spelling indicates that *Shekhinah* joins with *Yesod* (sixth day), in preparation for Her union with King *Tif'eret* on Sabbath eve. Disciples of the wise knowing that the divine couple unites every Sabbath eve, imitate the practice.[11]

The exile of *Shekhinah* extends throughout the fifth millennium, symbolized by Her letter *he*, whose numerical value is five. The world was created less than 6000 years ago on 3761 BCE. The fifth millennium corresponds to 240-41 CE to 1239-40 CE. The sixth millennium symbolized by the letter *vav*, whose numerical value is six, begins in the year 1240-41 CE. The seventh millennium, the cosmic Sabbath, beginning in 2240-41 CE is the Messianic era described as the day that is entirely Sabbath. *Tif'eret*, symbolized by *vav* that numerically equals six, ascends to *Hokhman*, symbolized by the *yod* of YHVH numerically equaling ten. Empowered by this ascent, He then descends to *Shekhinah*, symbolized by *he* numerically equaling five, and raises Her.[12]

> G-d rules the entire world, but He designated seventy heavenly princes to govern the other nations, whereas only Israel is ruled directly by Him.[13]

The flow of emanation, pictured as dew, descends from *Keter*. This sublime realm is characterized by pure compassion and is described as *arikh anpin*, 'slow to anger.' (Exodus 34:6) The *sefirot* from *Hokhmah* through *Yesod* is characterized by a tension between opposites: right and left, loving-kindness and judgment. Relative to the highest realm, this configuration is described as *ze'eir anpin*, 'short tempered.' (Proverbs 14:17) The emanated dew gradually reaches *Shekhinah*, the Holy Apple Orchard. The three Sabbath meals correspond to the three *sefirotic* realms: the Holy Ancient One, the Short-Tempered, and the Holy Apple Orchard. One who omits a meal impairs its corresponding divine aspect; one who completes all three meals demonstrates and actualizes the entire spectrum of faith.[14]

The day that is Shabbat to YHVH refers to the world that is coming. 'The seventh day' may refer to the seventh millennium, based on the tradition in BT Sanhedrin 97a in the name of Rabbi Katina: 'The world will exist for six thousand years and for one thousand lie desolate.'[15]

The twelve stones affixed to the breastplate symbolize the twelve boundaries associated with *Tiferet*, who is symbolized by Torah. These twlve supernal entities issue from *Binah*, a single subtle voice conveying divine will and thought. Below, are twelve others, namely the camps of angels, who issue from *Shekhinah*, another voice, who enunciates the divine word.[16]

On the Temple altar five things were reported about the fire of the pile of wood:

- it crouched like a lion;
- it was as clear as sunlight;
- its flame was of substance;
- it devoured wet wood like dry wood;
- it caused no smoke to rise.[17]

Within *Hokhmah* preexist all of the lower *sefirot*. The thirty-two paths of *Hokhmah* represent the twenty-two letters of the Hebrew alphabet and the ten *sefirot*. *Hokhmah* emanated a flow through these thirty-two paths, which gathered to form the one place of *Binah*. Ten *sefirotic* crowns emerged from the thirty-two paths, leaving twenty-two. Then these twenty-two paths (or letters) reached *Binah* and were engraved on Her fifty gates, yielding a total of seventy-two, corresponding to the divine name of seventy-two letters.[18]

> On the Sabbath seven men are traditionally called up to the Torah (plus an additional man). This number corresponds to the number of heavenly voices heard at Mount Sinai and to the seven *sefirot* from *Hesed* through *Shekhinah*. On holidays five are called up to the Torah (plus an additional one), perhaps corresponding to the five *sefirot* from *Hesed* through *Hod*, or to *Gevurah* through *Yesod* (all beneath the primordial light of *Hesed*). The six who are called up to the Torah on Yom Kippur correspond to the six *sefirot* from *Hesed* through *Yesod*, which are also known as the 'six directions.' These six are equivalent to the five *sefirot* from *Hesed* through *Hod*, since *Yesod* includes them all.[19]

The three consecutive months Nisan, Iyyar, and Sivan symbolize Abraham, Isaac, and Jacob (and their corresponding *sefirot*). Jacob synthesized the qualities and months of both Abraham and Isaac, so his month Sivan is ruled by Gemini (Twins). Esau, who strayed to the demonic realm, obtained only the next two months, Tammuz and Av; lacking the balance of the third month (Elul), he is unstable and his dominion transitory. Torah was given to Israel in the third month (Sivan), which is ruled by Gemini and combines the qualities of the two preceding months (Nisan and Iyyar).[20]

The arrangement of the twelve tribes in the wilderness of Sinai corresponds to the twelve oxen underneath the sea and to the various *sefiotic* limbs. Three tribes correspond to the right arm (*Hesed*), three to the left arm (*Gevurah*), three to the right leg (*Netsah*), and three to the left leg (*Hod*). *Shekhinah* rests above them. The three tribes in each direction correspond respectively to the three joints in each limb. The joints of the arm are the shoulder, elbow, and wrist; the joints of the leg are the hip, knee, and ankle. *Shekhinah* rests upon the twelve tribes, comprising together a holy structure of thirteen. The seventy members of the Sanhedrin symbolize the seventy angelic powers through which She sees and conducts the world.[21]

The Second Temple was destroyed in 70 CE Twelve hundred years later around the time of the Zohar's written composition in the 13th century the exile intensifies, until finally redemption begins to dawn 66 years later. Ergo the exile intensifies in 1270 or 1268 and redemption dawns in 1336 or 1334. However if 1200 years is intended as a round number the intensification of the exile corresponds with the beginning of the sixth millennium in 1240 CE (Hebrew 2239-40). The world was created less than 6,000 years ago at a date corresponding to 3761 BCE The 66 derives from the letter vav in YHVH (numerical value of 6 corresponding to *Tiferet* and the five other *sefirot* from *Hesed* through *Yesod* associated with Him). *Tiferet* is described as 'soul of the house of Jacob' or essence, of *Shekhinah* who contains or houses *Tiferet*, symbolized by Jacob. *Shekhinah* is symbolized by the *bayit sheni* (Second Temple or literally Second House) and the final lower *he* of YHVH.[22]

The name *Levi* is interpreted according the root *lvh* meaning to accompany or join. Levi also suggests Leviathan, who represents joy of union, Leviathan symbolizes *Yesod* (the *sefirah* of sexual union and pleasure), described as a river issuing from *Hokhmah* and *Binah*. Three months are characterized by harsh judgment: On the seventeenth of Tammuz, the walls of Jerusalem were breached; on the ninth of

Av, the First and Second Temples were destroyed; on the tenth of Tevet, the Babylonian siege of Jerusalem began.

Every seven sabbaticals is a Jubilee, proclaimed every 50 years, when slaves are released and the land reverts to its original owner. In kabbalah the Jubilee symbolizes *Binah* (mother of *Shekhinah*), who in general is characterized by the number 50. The colors white and black may symbolize *Hesed* and *Gevurah*, both of which issue from *Binah* and flank Moses' *sefirah*, *Tif'eret*.[23]

Every seventh year is a Sabbatical (*shemittah* or release) during which the land must lie fallow and at the end of which all debts are remitted. (Leviticus 25:1-24; Deuteronomy 15:1-3) In kabbalah the Sabbatical symbolizes *Shekhinah*, seventh of the lower *sefirot*. In the biblical cycle, after seven Sabbaticals comes the Jubilee, proclaimed every fifty years, when slaves are released and land reverts to its original owner. (Leviticus 25:8-55) The Jubilee symbolizes *Binah*, and is characterized by the number fifty, based on fifty gates of *Binah* (understanding) were created in the world, all of which were given to Moses except for one, as is said: "You made him little less than G-d." (Psalms 8:6) *Binah* is the source of redemption and liberation, specifically the Exodus from Egypt.[24]

Just as the seventh year (*shemittah*) releases one year in seven (by letting the earth lie fallow), so the world releases one millennium in seven (by being fallow and desolate). According to early kabbalah the world is destroyed every six millennia, lies in desolation for one millennium, and is then recreated anew and differently. "For a thousand years in Your eyes are like yesterday gone by." (Psalms 90:4) Seven such cycles culminate in the *yovel*, the cosmic Jubilee. The six thousand years comes from six days of creation in Genesis, the six words following the opening word of Genesis *(be-reshit)*, the six *sefirot* from *Hesed* through *Yesod* symbolized by the first six days of creation. In Kabbalistic theory of *Shemittot* each period of six millennia is dominated by one of the six *sefirot*. The sevens are linked like the sixes: the seventh millennium (above the previous six), the word *be-rehsit* (in the beginning) that is above or preceeding the following six words, or *Binah* that is above the six *sefirot*. When all ceases to exist in the seventh millennium, *Binah* will be exalted or fortified alone. Since the divine day (24 hours) is equivalent to a millennium, twelve hours refers to half a millennium. Ergo the first half of the seventh millennium will be destruction and the second half in the thirteenth hour a renewal of creation will be prepared by G-d where the thirteenth hour alludes to the thirteen attributes of Compassion, the thirteen enhancements of the divine beard, and the thirteen words of the second verse in Genesis not counting the first word.[25]

Various texts make note of seven heavens, seven earths, and seven seas. The Omer is seven weeks. The biblical Sabbatical and the Jubilee are seven years seven times. The Babylonian Talmud (BT Sanhedrin 97a) discusses the seven thousand years that the world will exist; it will exist for six thousand years and for one thousand lie desolate. In discussing that the blessed Holy One is in the seventh of all may refer to the highest of the seven heavens, the highest of the seven earths, in the Sabbath day, and in the seventh millennium (YHVH will be exalted on that day. (Isaiah 2:11)[26]

"They came to Elim, where there were twelve springs of water and seventy date palms." (Exodus 15:27) The oasis at Elim corresponds to the cosmic tree: the twelve springs of water symbolize the 'twelve boundaries or potencies of the tree on four sides of the world (corresponding to the *sefirotic* quartet of *Hesed, Gevurah, Tif'eret,* and *Shekhinah).* The seventy date palms symbolize the seventy heavenly princes of the nations of the world, all of whom are nourished by the tree.[27]

The Torah was given in black fire upon white fire. Black symbolizes *Gevurah,* or *Din* (Judgment), on the left, through which Torah was revealed to Israel; but this divine aspect merged with the white of *Hesed* (Love) on the right, thereby alleviating the rigor of Judgment. The image of black fire on white fire is attributed to Rabbi Shim'on son of Lakish.[28]

Shekhinah, the last of the ten *sefirot* is known as "the speculum that does not shine" and is symbolized by the color black. She has no light of Her own but reflects the light of the other *sefirot*. Her partner, *Tif'eret*, is "the speculum that shines," symbolized by the color white. The union of this divine couple depends upon the arousal of *Shekhinah*.[29]

> In the light of a candle the dark light cleaving to the wick symbolizes *nefesh*, which cleaves to the body. The white light symbolizes *ruah* and provides greater illumination. The halo around the white flame symbolizes *neshamah*, the highest level of the soul. The light of the candle symbolizes not only the various levels of the soul but also their corresponding *sefirot*, namely, *Shekhinah* (black light), *Tif'eret* (white light), and *Binah* (invisible light).[30]

> The three divisions of Israelites . . . priests, Levites, and Israel . . . correspond to the *sefirotic* tyriad of *Hesed, Gevurah*, and *Tif'eret*, who are symbolized by the colors white, red, and green (or purple).[31]

Yarns dyed in various colors (violet, purple, and crimson) were woven into components of the Dwelling and the priestly garments. Violet symbolizes *Shekhinah*, while purple symbolizes Her partner, *Tiferet*. Here, Rabbi El'azar is apparently associating *tekhelet*, violet with the root *klh*, to destroy. *Shekhinah* is consuming fire, fiercer than other fire. The color *tekhelet* refers to a violet or bluish purple dye extracted from the gland of the *Murex trunculus* snail. Whoever fulfills the commandment of wearing the *tzitzit* (Numbers 15:38-40) is as though he greeted the face of *Shekhinah* for the *tekhelet* (the colored thread on the tassel of the garment) resembles the sea, and the sea resembles the sky, and sky resembles the Throne of Glory.[32]

> He could not enter the Holy of Holies on Yom Kippur unless he was clothed in holy garments, which derived from the angelic garments worn by the celestial high priest Michael. Violet symbolizes *Shekhinah*, while purple (which comprises many colors) symbolizes *Tiferet*, who blends the polar opposites *Hesed* and *Gevurah* (symbolized respectively by white and red). Similarly, the complete name, YHVH Elohim, symbolizes the union of *Tiferet* and *Shekhinah*. The components of crimson . . . red

and violet . . . apparently symbolize *Gevurah* and *Shekhinah*.[33]

The epod was apparently a multicolored apron worn by Aaron the high priest. Its two shoulder straps bore two precious stones, each engraved with the names of six of the twelve tribes. Fastened to the ephod was breastpiece made of the same multicolored fabric, to which were affixed twelve other gemstones, each engraved with one of the names of the tribes.[34]

The ephod symbolizes *Shekhinah*, while the breastpiece symbolizes *Tif'eret*. Their being attached to each other symbolizes the union of the divine couple. The twelve stones affixed to the breastpiece and engraved with the names of the twelve tribes symbolize twelve boundaries, potencies, or lines branching out from *Tif'eret*, who is apparently identified as the place of existence. These twelve boundaries convey the flow of emanation and connect the lower *sefirot* to one another.[35]

The measurement of the linen curtains forming the innermost layer of the covering is holy, and its colors symbolize various *sefirotic* potencies. Apparently, the white linen symbolized *Hesed*; violet symbolizes *Shekhinah*; purple symbolizes *Tiferet*; and crimson symbolizes *Gevurah*. Whereas the dimensions of the linen curtains total thirty-two (corresponding to thrity-two paths of Wisdom), the dimensions of the goat-hair curtains total thirty-four, the numerical equivalent of the word *dal*, poor, alluding to the lack charactericstic of demonic forces.[36]

According to Exodus 39:27, the tunic worn by all the priests was made of *shesh*, linen. The word *shesh* can also mean six and according to rabbinic tradition, the linen yarn used in the Dwelling consisted of six strands. Here, six also alludes to the six *sefirot* from *Hesed* through *Yesod*, the first of which is symbolized by the priest. By wearing these garments of *shesh*, the priest is arrayed, as it were, in all *shesh sefirot*.[37]

The verse in Exodus about gazing at a rainbow actually refers to a vision of the rainbow whose colors convey the hidden *sefirotic* spectrum of *Shekhinah*.[38]

Each of the four elements is characterized by a pair of properties from among the contraries: hot and cold, wet and dry. Fire is hot and dry, water cold and wet, air hot and wet, and earth cold and dry. Further, fire is associated with *Gevurah* on the left side and with north; water is associated with *Hesed* on the right side and with south. North is the opposite of fire because it is characterized as cold and wet; these two opposites (north and fire) were blended, both symbolizing *Gevurah*. Similarly, south is the opposite of water because it is characterized as hot and dry; these two opposites (south and water) were blended, both symbolizing *Hesed*. G-d switched the hot and dry characteristics of fire to the south, from which heat issues to the world. Further, G-d blended water (cold and wet), so that water issues from the south and then enters the north (symbolizing *Gevurah*), from which it flows to the world. Fire on the left (*Gevurah*) and water on the right (*Hesed*) are in conflict, until *ruah* (wind, air, spirit) symbolizing *Tif'eret* mediates between them. Water, air, and the fire of the sun all provide essential ingredients to the dust of the earth, enabling her to yield vegetation. Similarly, all the three higher *sefirot* emanate into *Shekhinah*, enabling Her to generate life below.[39]

> When the cherubim in the Holy of Holies turn to face one another, *Shekhinah* turns from the blue of Judgment into a compassionate blend of white-greenish gold. White symbolizes *Hesed*; green signifies *Tif'eret*, also known as *Rahamin*

(compassion). Gold can symbolize *Binah,* source of both *Hesed* and *Tiferet.* According to BT Bava Batra 99a "Whenever Israel fulfilled the will of the Omnipresent," the cherubim in the Holy of Holies faced one another, and "whenever (Israel) did not," the cherubim miraculously turned away from each other toward the Temple courts.[40]

The primordial point of *Hokhmah* (symbolized by *yod*) generates the male and female couple, *Tiferet* and *Shekhinah,* symbolized respectively by *vav* and *dalet.* The full name of the letter *yod* includes these two letters, indicating the *Tiferet* and *Shekhinah* exist potentially within *Hokhmah.* The letters *dalet* and *vav* also spell the word *du* or two based on the Greek duo. This word appears in a famous Midrash describing the originally androgynous nature of Adam. *Yod* symbolizes Father *Hokhmah,* while *he* symbolizes Mother *Binah.* This *he* was originally *dalet,* before being impregnated by *Hokhamah,* after which *Binah* gave birth to *Tiferet,* symbolized by *vav.* This *vav* constitutes a new graphic element, or leg, transforming *dalet* into *he.* The full manifestation of *yod* (namely *Hokhmah*) includes both *he* and *vav* (namely *Binah* and *Tiferet*). The *vav* actually includes both *Tiferet* and *Shekhinah* (the lower Divine couple), and when these two unite, the *vav* 'settles,' covering and fulfilling the Divine Mother.[41]

The lovers in the Song of Songs are pictured as the divine couple, *Tif'eret* and *Shekhinah*. She sings praise to Her divine partner. Their union is expressed by the word *Haleluyah*. She is symbolized by *halelu* (praise) and He is indicated by the name *Yah* (often applied to *Hokhman* and *Binah*). The normal spelling of the biblical word for heart is *lev*, with one *vet*; the double *vet* symbolizes the two impulses (good and evil); "With all (*levavekha* . . . double *vet*) your heart." (Deuteronomy 6:5) The various members of the community are linked with specific *sefirotic* rungs. Priests and Levites symbolize respectively *Hesed* and *Gevurah*. Righteous and devout symbolize respectively *Yesod* and the pair *Netsah* and *Hod*. The upright refers to *Tif'eret* (the cental column), and assembly alludes to *Shekhinah*, who is known as *El*, G-d as in the phrase the assembly of G-d. Thus through their varied acts of worship, study, and righteous living, the people of Israel adorn G-d.[42]

Judah was progenitor of the Davidic dynasty, befitting his link with *Shekhinah* or *Malkhut* (Kingdom). Judah's name, *Yehudah* appears to contain the divine name. The first three letters (*yod, he, vav*) themselves constitute the holy name *Yaho*. The *yod* symbolizes *Keter* and the primordial point of *Hokhman*; the feminine marker *he* symbolizes Divine Mother, *Binah*; the *vav* (whose numerical value is six) symbolizes

Tif'eret together with the five *sefirot* surrounding Him (*Hesed* through *Yesod*). The divine name is completed by the next two letters in the name of *yehudah*: *dalet* and *he* both of which symbolize *Shekhinah*. The numerical value of *dalet* is four, which may allude to *Shekhinah's* role as fourth leg of the throne. Further, *dalet* suggests *dallah*, poor that describes *Shekhinah*, who has nothing of Her own, only what She receives from the *sefirot* above Her. When She is fully united with them, this *dalet* transforms into the second *he* of YHVH. The *dalet* serves as a link or knot joining the letters *yod, he, vav* with the second *he*. This image derives from the tradition that the knot of the *tefillah shel rosh* (phylactery worn on the head) is in the shape of the letter *dalet*.[43]

The *lamed* in the word *lo* (you shall have) stands taller than all other letters of the alphabet, indicating that G-d alone should be exalted and honored. The image of the upright *lamed* indicates one should not bow down to any false god. (Levitics 19:4) The *alef* or the concluding letter in *lo* has a numerical value of one, indicating G-d's oneness and unity, which must not be compromised or betrayed.[44] "The letter *qof* alludes to the demonic realm, perhaps because it begins the *qelippah* (husk), *qelalah* (curse), *qof* (ape), or conceivably because its numerical value (100) is equivalent to *samekh, mem*, an abbreviation of *Samma'el* (Samael), another name for

Satan. The demonic force, which generates evil and slander, is incompatible with the goodness of *tet*. Consequently, whenever the letter *tet* appears in the Bible, the letter *qof* cannot immediately follow (within the same word). According to the venerable source Rav Hamnuna Sava *het* and *tet* imply *hata'ah*, sin, which explains why these two letters do not appear in any of the names of the twelve tribes. Those names were engraved on the two carnelian stones of the high priest's ephod and on the twelve jewels of his breastpiece.[45]

The three lines in the letter *bet* symbolize the three *sefirotic* lights (*Hesed, Gevurah,* and *Tiferet*) or the three *sefirot* columns: right, left, and center. As the opening letter of the Torah *bet* includes all the components of *Tiferet*, who symbolizes Torah.[46]

Aaron was commanded to offer a calf in order to atone for the sin of the Golden Calf, which he had fashioned. This grave sin was an attempt to displace *Shekhinah* (symbolized by an unblemished cow) who has an eightfold nature corresponding to the high priest's eight garments. The garments included the four garments worn by all the priests: tunic, sash, headdress, and breeches. The four garments worn by only the high priest were ephod, breastpiece, robe, and gold medallion.[47]

In the Zohar Elisheba and Bathseheba were both destined to be married to Aaron and King David since both symbolize the same *sefirah*. The name *Bat Sheva* (literally daughter of seven) alludes to *Shekhinah*, the daughter of *Binah* (who is known as Seven since she includes all seven lower *sefirot*). Because *Shekhinah* receives the flow of all seven *sefirot* (*Binah* through *Yesod*) and includes all seven *sefirot* from *Hesed* through *Shekhninah* Herself, She is called *Bat Sheva*. Elisheva is understood as "My G-d is Seven" alludes to *Shekhninah* who is pictured as Seven. Bathsheba symbolizes *Shekhniah* and was destined for King David who is intimately linked with *Shekhinah*, or *Malkhut* (Kingdom).[48]

The Book of King Solomon interprets the phrase *asher ehyeh*, that I am, as alluding to the joyous, fruitful union of *Hokhmah* and *Binah*. The word *asher*, that, is associated with *osher*, happiness, namely the blissful bond between *Hokhmah* and *Binah* . . . who is alluded to as a "supernal castle." Having been impregnated by *Hokhmah*, *Binah* declares *Ehyeh*, I am (or I will be) for She is ready to give birth. "In blissful bond of a supernal castle" renders *be-qittura de-idduna qastira ila'ah*. *Qittura* is based on the root *qtr*, to tie, bind. *Idduna* is based on *iddun*, delight, and here alludes to *Hokhmah*, who is symbolized by *eden*, Eden meaning delight. *Qastira* derives from Latin *castrum (pl. castra)*, castle, fortress, military camp, and here symbolizes *Binah*, who is often pictured as a palace or house.[49]

CHARACTERS—FROM CREATION THROUGH 1200 CE

Primordial

Tohu and *bohu* refer respectively to primordial matter and form. *Tohu* was seen as the root of evil and *bohu* was the origin of good.[1]

The letters of the Hebrew alphabet presented themselves to G-d two thousand years prior to creation and He took delight in them. In the Torah the letters and the making of the words have deep meaning about what they represent and what they mean to G-d and to us.[2]

Nachmanides (known as Ramban 1194-1270 CE) gives the reason why there are no vowel-points in a *Sefer Torah*: "Since the vocalization is the form and soul of the letters, a *Sefer Torah* is not pointed, for it contains all the ways and methods (of interpretation), both inner and outer, and they may all be interpreted through each and every letter, aspects within aspects, secrets within secrets, and it has no limit known to us . . . If a *Sefer Torah* were pointed it would have a limit and a measure, like matter that has received a specific form, and it could be interpreted only in accordance with the particular vocalization that each word had. But since *Sefer Torah* is complete and perfected with every kind of perfection, and since heaps upon heaps of interpretations are carried out by every single word, it is not pointed, so that it can be interpreted in accordance with every kind of perfection and so that one may say, 'Do not read thus. Read thus.' This means that the spirit of the Torah hovers over the unvocalized letters and words, which are like primeval matter without any form. And the secrets of the Torah are revealed to the kabbalist through the many different ways in which he can read the words.³

> He sees at once that one should not add to these things or subtract from them. The real meaning of the text of Scripture is then revealed (from which) one should not add or subtract even a single letter. Therefore men ought to take note of the Torah and pursue her, and become her lovers, as I have explained.⁴

In Psalms 69:14 the donkey driver says "As for me, may my prayer to You, O YHVH, come at a time of favor . . ." A time of favor is when the congregation prays. By praying together as a congregation it adorns and enhances *Shekhinah* (known as time), preparing Her for union with *Tiferet* and transforming Her into a 'time of favor.' Such a time is propitious for presenting a request in prayer. *Shekhinah*, known as *Malkhut* (Kingdom), is symbolized by King David. Further, She is known as the Redeeming Angel and when She is joined with *Yesod*, who marries or 'redeems' Her, She is called Redemption. Finally, She is also called Prayer, since She conveys prayers to the higher *sefirot*.

In the daily morning liturgy, the blessing 'Blessed are You, YHVH, who has redeemed Israel' immediately proceeds the *Amidah*, the 'standing prayer via silent meditation' so central that it is known simply as Prayer. It is considered meritorious to join the blessing of Redemption to this prayer without any interruption or pause. Here, the joining of Redemption to Prayer is seen as the beginning of the union of *Yesod* and *Shekhinah*, and thus a time of favor . . . time alluding to *Shekhinah*, and favor alluding to *Yesod*, who transmits the flow of the higher *sefirot*, originating in *Keter* (who is known as *Ratson*, 'Will, Favor'). In uttering this verse, the Psalmist King David sought to unify the divine couple.[5]

Shekhinah, symbolized by the moon, was filled with radiance of seventy divine names (or powers) from each of three higher *sefirot: Hesed, Gevurah,* and *Tiferet.*[6]

The word *Va-ani* (and or as for me) signifies both *Yesod* and *Shekhinah. Yesod* is symbolized by the letter *vav*, whose numerical value is six, alluding to the six *sefirot* from *Hesed* through *Yesod* itself. *Shekhinah* is known as *ani*, I or me because through Her the divine personality reveals itself, declaring 'I am.'

The river in Genesis 2:10 issuing from Eden to water the Garden is understood to mean the river of emanation waters the garden of *Shekhinah* and from there divides. Genesis verses name the rivers: Pishon, Gibon, Tigris, Euphrates.

Seven halls (*hekhalot*) are situated below the *sefirot* and act as a kind of bridge between forces of emanation and the material cosmos. In relation to the upper world they are seen as the 'garments' of the *sefirot*, for in each of them a particular *sefirah* is revealed and active. They are numbered from bottom to top: *livnat ha-sapir* (sapphire pavement)/*Yesod,* perhaps including *Malkhut; ezem ha-shamayim* (the essence of heaven) or Zohar (radiance)/*Hod; nogah* (brightness)/*Nezah; zekhut* (merit)/*Gevurah; ahavah* (love)/*Hesed; razon* (good will)/

Tiferet; *kodesh* has—*kodashim* (holy of holies)/*Binah*. The halls are populated by hosts upon hosts of spirits, lights, creatures, wheels, seraphim, and other angels, which radiate light and which are linked to one another. They all yearn to be united with their Master. In every hall there is a supernal spirit at the head of the hosts within it, and he is the prince of the hall. These halls are residences of the supernal Garden of Eden where the souls take their delight after death. Parallel to these are seven halls in the lower Garden of Eden where Adam dwelt before sin caused his downfall.[7]

The Garden, Adam and Eve to Noah

Invalid prayers, slander, angry words, belligerent deeds, and other things of this kind reach the 'the other side' and strengthen its power. Metaphorically the strength is in restoring legs to the snake whose legs were cut off for seducing Adam and Eve in the Garden. When there is no one to support the Torah properly the supports are weakened and he who has no legs or feet to stand on is strengthened. The soul is part of the divine realm above, a spark emanated from the splendor of the *sefirot*. When the 'other side' gains control of any part of the sparks it actually subjugates part of the holiness of G-d. If the amount of sin actually tilts the balance of judgment in favor of conviction, the 'other side' seizes pure souls that have yet to descend into the physical world.

A wheel that stands at the door of the *Shekhinah* upon which souls go up and down portrays the mythical act. "On the pillar set aside for the scales, amid the air that blows, there are scales on one side, and other scales on the other side: scales of justice on one side, and scales of deceit on the other. And these scales never rest, but souls ascend and descend, enter and return. This world depends entirely upon the Tree of Knowledge of Good and Evil, and the tree dips toward good or evil depending on how people of the world are acting. When dipping toward evil it torments and seizes all the souls that happen to be in the scales at that time. The fate of these souls is determined in accordance with the interrelationship of the powers of good and evil in the conduct of the world. When the *Shekhinah* is weak and 'other side' is strong the souls are snatched away from the domain of holiness; i.e., they suffer because of the sins of mankind. In this situation the 'other side' is in a strong position to realize its main desire . . . to penetrate the realm of the *Shekhinah* and to subjugate Her.[8]

In kabbalah both the apple orchard and the Garden of Eden symbolize *Shekhinah*. She is filled with apple trees, namely, the *sefirotic* triad of *Hesed, Gevurah,* and *Tiferet,* who are symbolized by the three patriarchs and whose respective colors all appear in the apple: the white pulp, the red skin, and the green stem.[9]

Two powers of the chariot: the cherubim have a place next to the *Shekhinah* and they make music with their wings in her honor during the three watches of the night. The *hashmal* (electrum) is portrayed as sparks of flashing and dancing light that cannot be assigned a single fixed form. It is through them that prophetic visions are revealed. Only Moses was worthy to look upon these visions. The supernal speech, through which hidden mysteries are revealed, also emerged by way of *hashmal*.

The *Shekhinah* is called the *Pardes* of the Torah . . . She comprises the *peshat, re'ayah, derash,* and *sod* which makes the mnemonic *Pardes*. The four ways of interpreting the Torah are the four rivers that branched out of the river that flowed from Eden. The Torah (outline of *Sefirot*) has a head, body, heart, mouth, and organs just as Israel has. Israel is the wick, the Torah is the oil, and the *Shekhinah* is the flame.[10]

> When the serpent copulated with Eve, he injected her with *Zohama* (filth or slime, lust). Genesis 35 'The serpent-rider (Samael) copulated with her and she conceived Cain. Afterward her husband, Adam copulated with her and she conceived Abel.' Elsewhere the Zohar indicates that Cain was formed from both the serpent's slime and Adam's seed. From the fallen angel Samael (identified with the serpent),

Cain inherited traits of the upper world; from Adam he inherited traits of the lower world. Cain's demonic heredity influenced him to murder his brother, like a snake lurking in the field and striking suddenly.[11]

Bereshit Rabbah 19:7, in the name of Rabbi Abba son of Kahana: 'The root (or essence) of *Shekhinah* was in the world below. Once Adam sinned, She withdrew to the first heaven, Cain sinned; She ascended to the second heaven. The generation of Enosh sinned; She ascended to the third. The generation of the Flood sinned . . . to the fourth. The generation of the Dispersion . . . to the fifth. The Sodomites . . . to the sixth. The Egyptians in the days of Abraham . . . to the seventh.'

The sin of Adam is that the Tree of Knowledge of Good and Evil symbolizes *Shekhinah*. Adam's sin was that he worshiped and partook of *Shekhinah* alone, splitting Her off from the other *sefirot* and divorcing Her from her husband, *Tif'eret*, the Tree of Life. Psychologically the sin corresponds to the splitting off of consciousness from the unconscious.[12]

Adam and Eve's sons Cain (first) and Abel (second) were born after Eve copulated with the serpent and was infected by the serpent's slime thereby tainting both children. The demonic filth faded and the creative letters gave birth to Seth (third child) in which the letters of his name signify harmonious union of the divine couple: the three prongs of *shin* symbolize *Hesed, Gevurah,* and *Tiferet,* while *tav*, a feminine marker, symbolize *Shekhinah. Tiferet* and *Shekhinah*, in perfect accord, generated the pure soul of Seth.[13]

Moses de Leon (1250-1305 CE) in *Mishkan ha-Edut*, 63b says: "Because Adam did not want to wait until Sabbath eve (to unite with Eve) . . . evil and death came upon his descendants." According to BT *Ketubbot* 62b Sabbath eve is the appropriate time for scholars to engage in sexual union. In the Zohar, the union of the devotee of Torah with his wife on the eve of Sabbath symbolizes and stimulates the union of the divine couple, *Tiferet* and *Shekhinah*. The human couple thereby engenders a holy body and draws down a holy soul.[14]

By his sin Adam ruined the flow of emanation, pictured as a linguistic stream. The letters of the alphabet were reversed. By turning back to G-d he began to restore the letters to their proper order: the first two to be restored were *shin* and *tav*, which Adam named his son *Shet* or Seth. The process of alphabetic restoration was completed at Mount Sinai, when language manifested perfectly through the revelation of Torah, a renewal of the act of Creation.[15]

Enoch the unique man was able to achieve supernal perfection (the ideal) destined for all humanity and taken away by Adam's sin. Enoch purified himself of the material defects inherent in corporeal existence and advanced to the highest levels of angelic hierarchy. Enoch-Metatron symbolizes the culmination of the ascent that man is destined to strive; this refined image is superior to the angels.[16]

According to rabbinic tradition, the generation of the flood indulged in spilling semen (masturbation), a sin tantamount to murder since it wastes potential life. Although Genesis does not specify the nature of Er's sin, tradition maintains that it was identical with that of his younger brother, Onan (etymology of English words onanism and onanistic), who wasted (his seed) on the ground.[17]

The purpose of undeserved sufferings is to give the righteous additional merit and reward for withstanding great trials: "He tests the righteous in order to raise their standard, to display their eminence throughout the world." This type of trial is a descent into the realm of *sitra ahra*. Adam and Noah failed the test. When Adam saw the pleasures of the evil inclination he cleaved to it forgetting all that he perceived of the supernal glory of his Master. Noah descended and saw strong drink and became intoxicated uncovering himself.

Abraham and Isaac traveled to Egypt and the land of the Philistines and withstood all temptation. After Abraham entered the Promised Land he cleaved to *Shekhinah* and was granted *nefesh, ruah,* and *nehamah*. He was purified and returned to his place and became the right hand of the world. (Genesis 38:9)[18]

Abraham, Isaac, Jacob and Joseph

King Nimrod cast Abram into a fiery furnace. Terah, Abram's father was an idol worshipper and manufacturer (from Genesis 11:26-28 Terah's father was Nahor, son of Serug, descendants of Shem). Terah traveled somewhere and left Abram to sell in his place. A man approached, wanting to buy. Abram asked him how old he was and he said 50. He said: "Woe to such a man who is fifty years old and would bow down to an object one day old." Later a woman came carrying a plate of fine flour and told him to offer it to them. Abram took a stick and broke all the idols putting the stick in the hands of the largest. When his father returned asking who did this to them, Abram told him about the woman and fine flour and said each wanted to eat first so the largest took the stick and broke all of them. Terah said: "Why are you mocking me? Do they know anything?" Abram replied: "Don't your ears hear what your mouth is saying?" Terah seized him and took him to Nimrod. Nimrod said let us worship fire and they each replied one after the other with first Abram saying let us worship water which extinguishes fire. Let us worship clouds which carries water. Let us worship the wind which carries the clouds. Let us worship human beings, who withstand the wind. Nimrod ended saying you are playing with words. We will worship only fire. I will cast you into it, and let your G-d whom you worship come and save you. Abram's brother Haran was there but undecided as to whether to side with his brother or Nimrod. When Abram descended into the fiery furnace and was saved, Haran told Nimrod he sided with Abram. Haran was seized and cast into the fire and his innards were scorched, and he emerged and died in the presence of his father.[19]

Isaac was 37 when he was bound on the altar and Sarah died from anguish over her son's ordeal and Abraham came to mourn for her from Mount Moriah.[20]

Abraham purchased the cave of Machpelah as a burial site for Sarah. In Genesis 18:7 Abraham ran to fetch a calf for three messengers visiting him. The calf ran and entered the cave of Machpelah where he found Adam and Eve lying on their beds asleep, with lamps burning above them and a fragrant aroma around them . . . Therefore he desired to possess the cave of Machpelah as a burial site.[21]

Abraham's righteous conduct atones for Adam's sin, enabling him to ascend to his place in paradise.[22]

> Opposite these, seven righteous ones arose . . . Abraham, Isaac, Jacob, Levi, Kohath, Amram, Moses . . . and brought Her down to earth. Abraham, from the seventh to the sixth; Isaac brought (Her) down from the sixth to the fifth; Jacob brought (Her) down from the fifth to the fourth; Levi brought (Her) down from the fourth to the third; Kohath brought (Her) down from the third to the second; Amram brought (Her) down from the second to the first; Moses brought Her down below.[23]

Sarah was not the daughter of Terah, Abraham's father, but rather—according to rabbinic tradition—the daughter of Haran, Abraham's brother. Terah was the son of Nahor, the son of Serug, who descended from Shem's son Arpachshad.[24]

A ritual in which several animals were cut in half marked the covenant enacted between G-d and Abraham. Toward sunset, G-d spoke to Abraham: "Know well that your seed will be strangers in a land not theirs and they will be enslaved and afflicted four hundred years. But upon the nation that they serve I will bring judgment, and afterward they will go forth with great substance." (Genesis 15:13-14) It was part of a cosmic plan for Joseph to be sold into slavery by his brothers.[25]

From the time Isaac's birth is predicted in Genesis 18 until after the death of Abraham, Ishmael is not mentioned by name but is referred to simply as: son of the maidservant, son of Hagar, his son, boy, lad. (Genesis 21:9-20) Gold symbolizes Isaac and his corresponding *sefirah*, *Gevurah*, while dross symbolizes Ishmael and the forces of evil left over after the refining process of emanation. Exodus 32:6 teaches that Sarah saw Ishmael building idolatrous altars, catching locusts, and sacrificing them.[26]

Abraham prepared wood, a knife, and fire when he was about to bind Isaac on the altar. (Genesis 22:6) The mystical interpretation of the Isaac's sacrifice: Isaac and the fire symbolize frankincense and *Gevurah* and Abraham symbolizes myrrh and *Hesed*. The fire of *Gevurah* clings to *Shekhinah*, generating smoke. Jacob symbolizes *Tif'eret*, who blends the ingredients of *Hesed* and *Gevurah*.[27] Isaac was 37 when he was bound on the altar and Sarah died from anguish over her son's ordeal and Abraham came to mourn for her from Mount Moriah.[28]

Jacob wrestled with the power of the left and integrated it with the right . . . therefore he attained the rung of *Tiferet*, the sun. *Netsah* is symbolized as one thigh of Primordial Adam, paired with *Hod*, the other thigh. Together they constitute the source of prophecy. When Jacob was wounded in one thigh, *Netsah* was weakened and prophecy was suspended until the time of Samuel who restored it.[29]

BT *Shabbat* 55b "Four died through the incitement of the serpent, namely: Benjamin the son of Jacob, Amram the father of Moses, Jesse the father of David, and Chileab the son of David." This view states they did not sin on their own but died only because of the sin of Adam and Eve, who were enticed by the serpent.[30]

King Messiah will appear in the land of Galilee. The son of David will not come until all souls in the body have been depleted. The body is the heavenly treasure house of unborn souls.[31]

Since Samael (primordial serpent) had injured Jacob's thigh, which symbolizes the source of prophecy, prophetic vision was limited. Obadiah's vision of Edom's ultimate punishment (destruction of the second Temple in 70 CE) was an exception.

Moses' prophetic prophecy was not affected since he was linked with the higher *sefirot Tif'eret*.[32]

Jacob refers to *Shekhinah* perhaps because she is the heel (*aqev*), i.e., the end of the flow of emanation. When Jacob settled in Canaan, the land was still inhabited by enemies: thus his new name, Israel, was inappropriate. After Jacob's descendants became a nation that was modeled on the divine qualities (such as *Hesed*, symbolized by priests: *Gevurah*, symbolized by Levites), they were known permanently as *benei Yisra'el*, literally, "children of Israel." Rachel died while giving birth to Benjamin, Jacob's twelfth son. At this point *Shekhinah* replaced Rachel as mistress of Jacob's household since She was fittingly arrayed by the twelve (future) tribes.[33]

When Dinah was raped by Shechem (son of Hamor) her brothers Simeon and Levi avenged the outrage by killing Shechem, Hamor, and all the males of the town. Dinah's brothers derived from the *sefirah* of *Din* (Judgment) and could therefore execute judgment against Shechem and Hamor (associated with the demonic power *hamor* = donkey). Each of the twelve tribes corresponds to one of the signs of the zodiac. Simeon (associated with Taurus the bull) attacked Hamor (associated with the demonic *hamor*, donkey) to prevent the union of the demonic pair, ox and donkey, who threatened to attack Jacob. The successful assimilation of Joseph (identified with the ox) in Egypt (identified with donkeys) empowered the Egyptians, who thereby enslaved the Israelites. Moses the Levite severed the connection between ox and donkey by removing the bones of Joseph during the Exodus.[34]

Benjamin was born in suffering and harsh judgment (left side) that had been decreed against Rachel who was linked with *Shekhinah* symbolized by the left and the west. Jacob restored Benjamin to the right side (south with lovingkindness); he thereby sweetened the harshness within *Shekhinah* (west) drawing Her to the right as well. Rachel linked to *Shekhinah* was more revealed so her death is recorded explicitly in the Torah and her burial place is by the road. (Genesis 35:19; 48:7) Leah symbolizes the concealed realm of *Binah* so her death is not recorded in the Torah and she was buried within the cave of Machpelah.[35]

Joseph's dream related to his brothers in Genesis 37:7 ("Look, we were binding sheaves in the field, and look, my sheaf arose and actually stood up, and look, your sheaves gathered around and bowed down to my sheaf!") took twenty-two years to be fulfilled, i.e., for Joseph's brothers to bow down to him in Egypt. If the brothers had interpreted the dream unfavorably for Joseph, it would have been fulfilled

Dan accompanied by Asher and Naphtali on the north. The rabbinic view is that the tribes camped and marched in the same square arrangement in which they camped.[38]

The tribes of Gad, Reuben and half of Manasseh never entered the Promised Land, settling instead in the Transjordan. Gad was born to Leah's maid Zilpah and had a lower status and rung. Likewise Reuben was Jacob's firstborn but because he slept with his father's concubine (and Rachel's maid) Bilhah, he was deprived of the rich flow of blessing and consequently lost the birthright, the kingship, and the priesthood.[39]

Tamar was married to Judah's first-born son Er. When Er died his brother Onan should have married Tamar (custom of levirate marriage) but he wasted his seed on the ground and failed to consummate the marriage. (Genesis 38:9) Shelah, the youngest brother grew up and when Tamar was not given to him as a wife she seduced her father-in-law, Judah and the act eventually brought many benefits to the world since Tamar and Judah's son Perez was the ancestor of Boaz, who together with Ruth engendered Obed, the grandfather of King David (Ruth 4:18-21) from whom the Messiah will be descended.[40]

Jacob's son Asher derives from *osher*, happiness and alludes to *Yesod* who joyously conveys the delights of emanation to accordingly. However, their spontaneous, hateful response (Will you really reign over us?) guaranteed that the dream would be actualized precisely that way: by Joseph's dominance. By verbally expressing this interpretation, they had sealed both their fate and his. Realizing what they had done to themselves, they hated Joseph all the more.[36]

Leah symbolizes the divine mother, *Binah*, who is enthroned on a chariot supported by the quartet of *Hesed, Gevurah, Tiferet,* and *Malkhut*. Leah's first four children symbolize the quartet of Reuben, Simeon, Levi, and Judah. Elsewhere the four symbolic supports of the chariot-throne are the patriarchs: Abraham, Isaac, and Jacob, joined by King David, who is descended from Judah. Judah's descent from royalty symbolizes the descent of *Malkhut* (Kingdom) once She is deprived of the nourishing flow from *Yesod*—a lack symbolized by Joseph's disappearance.[37]

Numbers 10:11-28 says the tribes journeyed through the wilderness in a single column, with Dan serving as the rear guard. The tribes camped in a particular fashion (Numbers 2:1-31). Judah accompanied by Issachar and Zebulun on the east, Reuben accompanied by Simeon and Gad on the south, the Levites carrying the ark in the middle, Ephraim accompanied by Manasseh and Benjamin on the west, and

Shekhinah, known as *Malkhut*. From a higher perspective Asher alludes to *Binah*, the Divine Mother and source of the delightful flow. She is called happy by her daughters, the lower *sefirot* who issue from Her. She is also symbolized by Leah, who, upon the birth of Asher, proclaimed herself happy.[41] After Jacob tricked his father Isaac into giving him the blessing of the firstborn, Esau wept bitterly. Those tears moved Hashem to reward Esau and his descendants with worldly blessing and dominion, including dominion over Israel. Esau symbolizes both the Roman Empire and medieval Christianity, both of which subjugated the Jewish people.[42] Jacob possessed the 'house below' in that he married Leah and Rachel along with their maids, Zilpah, and Bilhah so he never attained complete union with the 'house above,' the divine wife, *Shekhinah*, although as a result of his marriages he did array Her with the twelve tribes and his seventy descendants. Moses, on the other hand, after encountering G-d on Mount Sinai, abstained from sexual contact with his wife and maintained union with *Shekhinah*, becoming husband of *Elohim*.[43]

Rachel had two children Joseph and Benjamin who fathered three of the twelve tribes: Ephraim, Manasseh, and Benjamin. Leah had six children: Reuben, Simeon, Levi, Judah, Issachar, and Zebulun who fathered six tribes.[44] Caleb was the chieftain of the tribe of Judah, who, as progenitor of the Davidic dynasty, symbolizes *Malkhut* (Kingdom). By joining the patriarchs in Hebron, Caleb symbolized and actualized the union of *Malkhut* with *Hesed, Gevurah,* and *Tiferet*.[45]

The world stands upon three things: Torah, worship, and good deeds. Jacob is Torah, Isaac is worship, and Abraham is good deeds.[46] Rabbi Shim'on identifies the column of cloud with Abraham (who symbolizes *Hesed*) and column of fire with Isaac (who symbolizes *Gevurah*). He supports Rabbi Abba's association of the cloud with *Yesod,* since through the rung of *Yesod* both cloud and fire (*Hesed* and *Gevurah*) appear in *Shekhinah*. At first, Isaac thought that the fragrance emanated from the garments; but then he sensed a paradisial fragrance, emanating from Jacob himself. Isaac knew the fragrance because the field he meditated was the field of the cave of Machpelah, which Abraham had purchased from the Hittites as his family burial site. Issac perceived *Shekhinah* hovering over the field and discovered Her fragrance; from then on, he prayed there daily. He also recognized the divine aroma from when he was bound on the altar at Mount *Moriyyah* which is named for *mor,* myrrh, alluding to the fragrance of *Shekhinah*. Abraham already had a fixed place for prayer. From this comes the belief that Abraham instituted the morning prayer, Isaac the afternoon prayer, and Jacob the evening prayer.[47]

In YHVH *Hesed, Gevurah,* and *Tiferet* are symbolized respectively by the first three letters, while the final *he* designates *Shekhinah*. Leah's first three sons (Reuben, Simeon and Levi) symbolize the triad of *Hesed, Gevurah,* and *Tiferet,* her fourth son, Judah—progenitor of the Davidic dynasty— symbolizes *Shekhinah,* or *Malkhut* (Kingdom).[48]

> As Jacob and Leah's firstborn son, Reuben symbolizes the first of the seven lower sefirot, *Hesed,* on the right. However, when he sinned by sleeping with his father's concubine Bilhah, he deviated to the left. Generations later, the tribes of Simeon and Gad (also associated with the left) journeyed together with the tribe of Reuben. Judah, on the other hand, began from the left and turned to the right, and so fittingly his descendant Bezalel made the Dwelling whose list of precious materials begins with gold (symbolizing *Gevurah* on the left) and then proceeds to silver (symbolizing *Hesed* on the right).[49]

Moshe: Salvery to Deliverance

Divine punishment can be suspended as in the story of the Golden Calf. Moshe did not intervene (as *Shekhinah* would have done) with *Hashem* when He accused Israel of acting corruptly. G-d prodded Moshe by saying "Now leave Me be, that My wrath may blaze against them and I may consume them, and I will make you a great nation." Moshe realizing it was on him to save Israel grabbed G-d's right arm by invoking Abraham, who symbolizes that arm, the divine quality of *Hesed*.[50] By constructing the Dwelling in the desert, Moses provided a temporary home for *Shekhinah* on earth. Later, Solomon united Her above with *Tif'eret* and invited both of them to dwell in the Temple that he built in Jerusalem. Further, he enhanced the gaze of *Binah* (the upper world), ensuring that *Shekhinah* (the lower world) would be enhanced. (Bereshit Rabbah 19:7)[51]

The Zohar portrays Abraham and Moses as righteous in the extreme. They petitioned for the deliverance of the wicked and sacrificed their own interests for them. Noah was a lower level of righteousness; he concerned himself with his own personal affairs and did not plead for his generation.[52]

> The *tsits*, medallion (or plate, rosette), was a gold plate worn on the forehead of the high priest over his turban, bearing the inscription *qodesh la'YHVH*, Holy to *YHVH*. Rabbi Shim'on relates the word *tsits* to the verbal root *tsuts*, to look, peek, peer, gaze. He

proceeds to explain how the *tsits* enabled the high priest to determine a person's character.[53]

The patriarchs saw the colors of the *sefirot* reflected in *Shekhinah* but could not gaze at them directly. Moses, attained fully the rung of *Tif'eret* (known as YHVH), who includes all of the *sefirot* from *Hesed* through *Yesod*. His vision of the colors was unmediated.[54] G-d appeared to his 'beloved friends' the patriarchs, by channeling words and visions through *Shekhinah*, who, before She was married, was known specifically as *El Shaddai*. Moses, however, had direct contact with G-d, attaining the rung of *Tif'eret* and uniting with *Shekhinah*.[55]

Life, children, and sustenance do not depend on merit but on *mazzala*, destiny. *Mazzala* can symbolize the Holy Ancient One (*Keter*). According to Rabbi Yitshak all of humanity's basic needs including nourishment and sexual partnership are as difficult as splitting the Red Sea because all of these needs as well as the miracle at the sea depend upon the same ultimate level: the Holy Ancient One.[56]

The Zohar denigrates with great severity those who occupy themselves with only the literal dimension of the Torah and do not strive to master the secret of the G-dhead concealed within it. The narratives in the Torah are like clothes; the commandments stand for the body, while the mystical doctrine is the soul. 'The fools in the world look only upon the clothes, which are the narratives of the Torah; they know no more, and do not see what is beneath the clothes. Those who know more do not look upon the clothes, but upon the body beneath the clothes. The wise, the servants of the supreme King, those who stood a Mt. Sinai, look only upon the soul, which is the foundation of all, the real Torah.' Maimonides depicts a ladder of perfection among men according to their nearness to, or remoteness from, G-d, in terms of a king sitting in a palace, with his subjects, who seek to enter his presence, divided into various categories according to the their position relative to the king's abode.[57]

He encompasses all worlds, and none He surrounds them on every side, above and below and in the four corners of the globe, and none may go beyond His domain. He fills all worlds, and no other fills them . . . He binds and joins the species with one another, above and below, and there is no juncture of the four elements except (by) the Holy One, blessed be He, existing among them.⁵⁸

Moses anointed Aaron because he is considered the son of *Binah*, the Divine Mother and Fountain of Life, who conveys the flow to *Hesed* (symbolized by Aaron) on the right. A verse in Isaiah implies that G-d sent Aaron, symbolizing *Hesed*, to be Moses' right hand.⁵⁹ Midrashic interpretation says Aaron's sons Nadab and Abihu died because they were not married.⁶⁰ Other reasons for the death of Nadab and Abihu were they were drunk, lacking the proper priestly garments, or had not washed their hands and feet, or had not fathered children. Rabbi Abba insists the reason is because they were not married which rendered them unfit to bring any offering especially incense, which surpasses all other offerings. They were not worthy of *Shekhinah*, much less of effecting the union of higher *sefirot*.⁶¹

Nadad and Abihu's brother Eleazar married Putiel, who then bore Phinehas who was to rectify the sin of Nadab and Abihu. The name Phinehas alludes to the fact that Nadab and Abihu's souls . . . which were not consumed by the divine fire . . . were later reincarnated in Phinehas. "What is to be already has been" since Phinehas was already born and named before Nadab and Abihu sinned, and he was prepared to correct their future flaw. The biblical clause may also allude to the eventual reincarnation of Nadab and Abihu in Phinehas.[62]

Exodus (14:19-21) combines a phrase to form a complex name deriving from three consecutive verses: "The angel of *Elohim* who was going before the camp of Israel moved and went behind them, and the column of cloud moved from before them and stood behind them. And it came between the camp of Egypt and the camp of Israel, and there was the cloud and the dark, and it lit up the night, and one did not draw near the other all night. And Moses stretched out his hand over the sea, and YHVH drove the sea with a mighty east wind all night, and He turned the sea into dry ground and the waters were split." In the Zohar *Shekhinah* is pictured as the angel of *Elohim* journeying along with Israel. According to tradition the 216 Hebrew letters composing the three verses are rearranged into 72 triads (known as the Name of Seventy-two) in the following pattern: the first letter of the first verse, the last letter of the second verse, the first letter of the third verse (forming one triad); the second letter of the first verse, the penultimate letter of the second verse, the second letter of the third verse (the second triad); etc.[63]

Joshua, First Temple, Saul, Solomon, David

Hesed, Gevurah, Tif'eret, and *Shekhinah* are identified with the three patriarchs and King David forming a chariot for *Binah* and engender all the lower worlds and all created beings. From them issue four metals: gold from *Gevurah*, silver from *Hesed*, copper from *Tif'eret*, and iron from *Shekhinah*. Fire and north is linked with *Gevurah*, water and south with *Hesed*, Air and east with *Tif'eret*, dust and west with *Shekhinah*. The four elements, the four directions, and the four metals constitute a total of twelve aspects.[64] The entire Temple ritual stimulates the union of the divine couple above. The lamp of *Shekhinah* is kindled. The priest and the Levites symbolize respectively the right and the left arms, *Hesed* and *Gevurah*, which are also symbolized by water and wine. Wine is offered as a libation on the altar in the Temple (below) in order to bring about a mingling of *Gevurah* and *Hesed* above, thereby assuaging the harshness of the left.[65] Nimrod was King of Babylonia and Assyria (Genesis 10:8-12). According to legend, his spectacular success as a hunter derived from the fact that he wore the magic clothes fashioned by G-d for Adam and Eve. Seeing Nimrod in these clothes, Esau coveted them and killed him for them.[66]

According to BT Sotah 46b one enters the town of Luz in the land of the Hittites through the hollow of an almond tree, to a cave and into the town. That is the Luz in which they dye the blue (for *tsitzit*). That is the Luz against which Sennacherib marched without disturbing it (i.e., plundering it and exiling its inhabitants), against which Nebuchadnezzar marched without destroying it. And even the Angel of Death has no permission to pass through it, but when the old people there become weary of life (literally when their mind becomes loathsome to them) they go outside the wall and die.

The immortal city of Luz shares its name with the immortal bone of the human body supposed to be at the base of the spine. This bone, shaped like *luz* (an almond), is said to be indestructible, and from it G-d will one day resurrect decomposed bodies.[67]

King Nebuchadnezzar cast Joshua the high priest into the fire along with the false prophets Ahab, son of Kolaiah and Zedekiah son of Maaseiah. The two false prophets burned to death, while Joshua emerged with only his clothes singed.[68]

1 Samuel 21-22: David was fleeing from King Saul and comes to Nob and finds the priest Ahimelech, who provides him with bread and a weapon. In retaliation Saul orders the massacre of all the priests and inhabitants of Nob. In punishment for Saul's sin G-d sent Sennacherib to Nob and to destroy Jerusalem but the period of punishment expired since Sennacherib let his army rest planning to attack the next day when his forces were decimated by an angel. When the priests of Nob were killed *Shekhinah* was unable to unite with her spouse *Tiferet* and *Shekhinah* moved to the left, the side of harsh Judgment. Saul along with his sons and many Israelites were killed in the battle with the Philistines.[69] (Psalms 119:62 and Berakhot 3b): "Rabbi Shim'on the Hasid said, 'There was harp suspended above King David's bed. As soon as midnight arrived, a north wind came and blew upon it and it played by itself. He immediately arose and engaged in Torah until the break of dawn." In early medieval times this parallels the midnight vigil common among Christian monks.[70] King Messiah will appear in the land of Galilee[71]

The first Temple destroyed by the Babylonians in 586 BCE symbolizes the Divine Mother *Binah*. She is symbolized by the first *he* in the name YHVH. Grammatically, *he* is the typical feminine marker in Hebrew. The seventy-year exile of the first exile symbolizes the seven *sefirot* (*Hesed* through *Shekhinah*), which gestate within and issue from *Binah*. During that exile, *Binah* was estranged from those children, who were thus separated from Her name—indicated by the letter *he*. The *yod* is the first letter of YHVH and symbolizes the primordial point of *Hokhmah*, which waters *Binah*. Although normally united with *Binah*, during the first exile He withdrew above to *Ein Sof*. Consequently, *Binah* (known as the First Temple) could no longer convey the stream of emanation to the lower *sefirot*. When the exile ended not all Jews returned to Israel or turned back to G-d. Even though the end of exile signified the empowerment of *Shekhinah* who is symbolized by the final (lower) *he* of YHVH Israel's sporadic behavior impeded the emanation from *Hokhmah*, symbolized by *yod*. Their imperfection strengthened the forces of harsh judgment on the left, which constricted the flow.[72]

> In the realm of Holiness, fewer letters actually signify an addition. As an example, Rabbi Abba refers to the large bronze reservoir built by Solomon in the Temple, which rested on twelve bronze oxen, three facing outward in each direction. This reservoir symbolizes *Shekhinah*, who is arrayed by twelve angelic forces beneath Her. Here the abbreviated

spelling *shenei asa*, twelve . . . rather than the full spelling *sheneim asar* indicates the full holiness of Shekhinah.[73]

According to the account in Kings (20:8-11) and Isaiah (38:7-8) King Hezekiah asked Isaiah for a sign that he would be healed, and G-d made the shadow of the royal sundial recede ten steps. Rav Huna (Midrashic souces) relates on that day King Merodach-Baladan, the Babylonian King (who usually slept five hours from 10 AM to 3 PM apparently slept instead for ten hours, yet when he awoke it seemed not like 8 PM but 10 AM since time had gone ten hours backward. Mistakenly he thought he slept an entire day and became angry at his soldiers.[74]

Soul, body, spirit, actions

The Torah is compared to wheat. The four forms of wheat (kernels, bread, cake, and royal pastry) represent four levels of meaning: simple, midrashic, allegorical, and mystical. Simple learning is superficial unless it flowers into all it can be. Rather than reducing the unknown to the familiar, one should savor the variety of possible meanings. There is a parable of a king with two servants who he gives each a measure of wheat and a bundle of flax. The foolish servant did nothing. The wise servant made cloth to cover the baked bread he made from the wheat. When G-d gave Torah he gave it as wheat from which to produce fine flour, and as flax from which to produce cloth.

> Maimonides (Guide of the Perplexed 1:31): A person has in his nature a love, and an inclination from that to which he is habituated. Thus you can see that people of the desert . . . notwithstanding the disorderliness of their life, the lack of pleasures, and the scarcity of food . . . dislike the towns, do not hanker after their pleasures, and prefer the bad circumstances to which they are accustomed to good ones to which they are not accustomed. Their souls accordingly would find no repose in living in palaces, in wearing silk clothes, and in the enjoyment of baths, ointments, and perfumes.

In a similar way, a person has love for, and the wish to defend, opinions to which he is habituated and in which he has been brought up and has a feeling of repulsion for opinions other than those. For this reason also a person is blind to the apprehension of the true realities and inclines toward the things to which he is habituated. This happened to the multitude with regard to the belief in His corporeality and many other divine subjects as we shall make clear. All this is due to people being habituated to, and brought up on, texts that it is an established usage to think highly of and to regard as true and whose external meaning is indicative of the corporeality of G-d and of other imaginings with no truth to them, for these have been set forth as parables and riddles.[75]

In every area of the Zohar it is stressed that activity in the *sefirotic* world above depends on human involvement below in holy deeds and holy speech. Deeds above are aroused by deeds below, and the deed below must appear as a model of the deed above. If a man performs a deed below correctly, a power is aroused correctly in the world above. With an image of a lamp the *Shekhinah* is the lamp, man's body is the wick, and his good deeds are the oil that fuels the lamp. When the channels are functioning correctly there is a harmonious balance between Judgment and Love . . . male and female powers are joined together. He who walks in G-d's path creates Him, as it were, in the world above. Man continually renews upper world creation by sustaining the *sefirotic* system. Neglect of the commandments hinders the channels and hinders the flow of influence and the 'other side' is allowed to become involved in the web of human activity.[76]

Male and female on their own are imperfect separate parts. The married state represents the whole and perfect human condition. When together they represent unity, one body, and the celestial Adam. When not united they each represent half a body, or half a soul. Souls prior to descending to the physical world are bisexual and before they enter their respective bodies their attending angel is in charge of conception. Priests must be married or they are considered blemished and cannot conduct the ceremonies.[77]

Neglecting "to bear fruit and multiply" stops the river from flowing and damages the holy covenant on all sides. The childless man is barren and dies in this world and the world to come . . . it is as if he were never created . . . his soul cleaves to *'sitra ahra.'* Those that are childless must be reborn by means of transmigration of the soul in order to make good this defect. The childless soul is punished in *Gehinnom* before it transmigrates and redeems itself. It gets three chances at redemption after which it has no further chance and he shall surely be cut off.[78]

BT Bava Batra 16b: "Do you observe the calving of does (Job 39:1). This doe has a narrow vagina. When she crouches to give birth, I prepare a serpent who bites the vagina and she is loosened of her offspring. If it comes one second too soon or one second too late, she immediately dies." Here the doe symbolizes *Shekhinah*, who gives birth to human souls. The splitting of Her womb parallels the splitting of the Red Sea (which also symbolizes *Shekhinah*). The demonic serpent plays a mysterious and vital role in the birth process, and Rabbi Shim'on insists that one should not probe the matter any further. Rabbi Abba teaches that the demonic serpent bites the doe's vagina twice. After the first bite, the serpent licks her blood, deriving nourishment; after the second bite, water issues, sustaining heavenly creatures. The serpent's bite and the nourishment that he derives ensure a successful birth, which sustains life in the worlds below.[79]

PLACES/THINGS—GARDEN OF EDEN, MACHPELAH, BABEL, CLOUD, FLOOD

Primordial—Sefirot

The principal terms used for the divine *sefirot (sefirot* of holiness) are abstract ideas and indicate spiritual forces, emotional attributes, or qualities of exaltation. They are not individual people but are general archetypes, overall categories for specific entities. Motherhood and fatherhood are in perfection as *Hokhmah* and *Binah*. When describing male and female in the G-dhead they are the essence of maleness and femaleness. It is stated that "all the females of the world exist in the mystery of the *Shekhinah*." She is the divine archetype of eternal womanhood that is actually embodied and realized in the particular personalities of mortal women.

The Leviathan is the primordial sea monster who, together with his mate, threatened the world until they were vanquished by G-d. In the time to come, the righteous will feast at a banquet, and their main course will be Leviathan's female partner. Rabbi Shim'on begins to describe the demonic realm, comprising ten sea serpents swimming in ten rivers, corresponding to the divine realm of ten *sefirot*. The chief demonic power . . . the great sea serpent . . . sprawls in nine rivers but returns again and again to the calm river, which is fed by the waters of *Shekhnah*, the Garden. Thus the demonic realm is nourished and sustained by the divine.[1]

At wedding ceremonies under the *Chuppah* there are six blessing preceded by the blessing over the wine. The wine in the first blessing symbolizes the flow from *Binah* to *Shekhinah*, who is symbolized by the vine. The arousal of divine passion is initiated by *Gevurah* on the left; then *Hesed*, the right arm embraces *Shekhinah*, and *Yesod* or *Tif'eret* (the Tree of Life) unites with Her. The second blessing praises G-d who has created all for His glory. 'All' symbolizes *Yesod*, the divine phallus and the site of the covenant of circumcision, who conveys the entire flow of emanation, which courses through the various *sefirotic* limbs, to *Shekhinah* (symbolized by the vine and glory). The flow originates in *Binah* and appears first in *Hesed* on the right before continuing to *Yesod*. The fruitlessness of the left side is related to the impotence of the demonic realm, which is rooted in the left. The third blessing praises G-d for creating *ha-adam*, the human being and refers to *Tiferet* who harmonizes the polar opposites *Hesed* and *Gevurah* that constitutes the trunk of the *sefirotic* body (mystery of Adam). *Tiferet* is also symbolized by Jacob, who embodied the primordial beauty and power of Adam. The fourth blessing is about the human being created in the divine image and corresponds to the right thigh. The fifth blessing is linked to the left thigh. The essence of the house is *Shekhinah* who delights in the ingathering of Her exiled children . . . but also constantly in the influx of new souls of Israel emanating from the *sefirot* above Her. The two divine thighs (*Netsah* and *Hod*) join together and gather these souls, bringing them 'between the knees' (also symbolizing *Netsah* and *Hod*). This *sefirotic* pair is the source of prophecy, and they provide joy to *Shekhinah* (essence of the house). They are also pictured as willow stems which do not themselves yield fruit; yet by gathering new souls from above, they convey fruit (via *Yesod*) to *Shekhinah*. *Netsah* and *Hod* are also pictured as two testicles, conveying seed to *Yesod*.[2]

Hallelujah comprises two elements: the divine name *Yah* and directive *halelu* (praise) and is the totality of the holy supernal Name. *Hallel* (praise) alludes to *Shekhinah* who constantly offers praise to the blessed Holy One and is symbolized by the final letter *he* of YHVH and the remaining letters of *haleluyah* consist of the rest of YHVH (*yod, he, vav*).³

According to rabbinic tradition, "whoever welcomes (literally receives the face of) the wise is considered as if he welcomes *Shekhinah*." . . . Whoever receives the face of his teacher/friend is considered as if he receives the face of *Shekhinah*." The Zohar transforms the rabbinic simile into an actual description of the righteous, who are called the face of *Shekhinah* "because *Shekhinah* is hidden within them: She is in concealment, they are revealed." (Zohar 2:163b)⁴

The Garden

Rabbi Abba had a dream and saw Rabbi Shim'on in which Shim'on explains that *Binah* is the river of emanation issuing from *Hokhmah* (symbolized by Eden). The primordial point of *Hokhman*, symbolized by the letter *yod*, encloses itself within *Binah* and then expands Her into the wide letter *he*. These are the first two letters of YHVH. Impregnated by *Hokhmah*, *Binah* gives birth to *Tif'eret* (together with the five *sefirot* surrounding Him, from *Hesed* through *Yesod*) symbolized by the letter *vav* whose numerical value is six. Fittingly, the shape of the letter *vav* corresponds to the left leg of the letter *he*, implying that this son begins within the womb of the Divine Mother. After His birth, the son is placed before Her to be suckled, a relationship depicted by the progression *he, vav,* the middle letters of YHVH.⁵

> The earthly Garden of Eden has its own special heaven. The heavens above most of the world were fashioned from fire and water. The blessed Holy One took *esh,* fire, and *mayim,* water, mixed them with one another and from them *shamayim,* heavens, were made. These heavens extended until the Garden of Eden, where they halted. Then, for the special heaven of the Garden itself, G-d took supernal fire and water (symbolizing *Gevurah* and *Hesed*) from *Tiferet* (known as heaven) and fashioned a more rarefied heaven, joined to the heaven of the world.⁶

> In relation to the earthly Garden, *Shekhinah* (the Lower Point) is Eden, the source of the river. However, in relation to the Higher Eden *Hokhmah, Shekhinah* is the Garden. In the verse from Isaiah, the phrase *Elohim zulatekha,* Oh G-d, but you, can be interpreted in two ways. It may refer to *Shekhinah* (the Lower Point) 'who is often called *Elohim* and

'who knows' (and is even identified with) this Eden below.' Alternatively, this divine name can signify *Hokhmah* (Highest Eden), who generates *Binah*, known as 'the World that is coming.' Since *Binah* too is often called *Elohim*, here the name may be applied to Her source, *Hokhmah*. The supernal *sefirah* of *Hokhmah* knows and joins *Shekhinah* by means of the river of *Yesod*.[7]

The river of *Yesod* streams soul into *Shekhinah* (the supernal Garden), who then gives birth to them, conveying them into physical bodies on earth. After departing from this world, the souls are refined and calmed by the 'river below' in the earthly Garden. Here on earth, a troubled person is often able to calm his soul by sitting by a river, since this recalls his soul's origin in the river of *Yesod*.[8]

Souls who are worthy and have been purified ascend through the column in the middle of the earthly Garden to the heavenly Garden. Inside the column is a glow, while cloud and smoke conceal the column and the souls within it from those souls remain in the Garden below.[9]

A soul that needs purification by fire is brought to a special place in Hell called *Gen-hinnom* which is a valley south of Jerusalem where child sacrifices were allegedly offered to Molech and also served to incinerate refuse, dump animal carcasses and the bodies of criminals. *Gen-Hinnom* serves as a purgatory, so that souls can be cleansed in fire and afterwards enter the Garden of Eden.[10]

> *Sefer Yetsirah* 6:1: When G-d created the sky above us, divided into seven heavens, He created the *teli*, dragon, out of fire and water in the form of a great serpent—like a great, sinuous snake. He gave it a head and a tail and placed it in the fourth heaven, the middle one, abode of the sun, and He stretched it from one end to the other like a bar, like a sinuous serpent . . . and all the stars, luminaries, and constellations are attached to it. As threads of warp and woof are attached to a weaver's beam, so all the stars in the seven heavens above and below are attached to it.[11]

. . . The forces of evil originate in the *sefirah* of *Gevurah*, or *Din* (Judgment), which expresses divine wrath. The smoke of this fiery wrath pushes outward, brakes through the boundary of holiness, and then spreads twistingly, dispersing evil. The emergence of the demonic point corresponds to the emergence of the primordial point of *Hokhmah*.

BT Berakhot 60b "When one hears the rooster crowing he should say: 'Blessed is He who has given the rooster understanding to distinguish between day and night.'" Here the rooster marks the moment of midnight, the beginning of the union of *Tif'eret* and *Shekhinah*. Pereq Shirah 2:57 "When the blessed Holy One comes to the righteous in the Garden of Eden, all the trees of the Garden sprinkle spices before Him. Then he (the rooster) praises."[12]

G-d divided the original androgynous human, Adam into two halves: male and female. Rabbi Yitshak locates them in the east and west respectively, corresponding to *Tif'eret* and *Shekhinah*.[13] According to a verse in Deuteronomy, *Tif'eret (ha-adam)*, the (divine) human, Primordial Adam . . . is a tree planted in the field of *Shekhinah*, who is Herself known as 'field of holy apples.' When besieging a town one is not to destroy its fruit trees.[14]

> When the serpent copulated with Eve, he injected her with *zohama* (filth, slime, lust). Israel, who stood at Mt. Sinai . . . their *zohama* ceased. Star-worshippers, who did not stand at Mount Sinai . . . their *zohama* did not cease.[15]

On Sabbaths and festivals the souls strip themselves of garments and ascend to the celestial Garden of Eden. The human being is created in the image dynamics of the *sefirot*. The highest divine spirit animates *Tif'eret* (known as spirit) and highest divine soul animates *Binah* (known as soul). As emanation proceeds, a spirit of *Yesod* (known as source of life) enters *Shekhinah* . . . who contains all souls, embodies all of the *sefirot*, and is called Body. *Yesod*, who contains the entire flow of the higher *sefirot* is also called all, providing all that is needed by the body of *Shekhinah*, as implied in the verse of Ecclesiastes: "The abundance of earth (symbolizing *Shekhinah*) is in all." Namely is contained in, and conveyed by, *Yesod*. The designation of *Shekhinah* as Body derives, at least in part, from a Talmudic teaching in the name of Rabbi Assi (BT Yevamot 62a): "The Son of David (i.e., the Messiah) will not come until all souls in the body have been depleted." 'The body' is the heavenly treasure-house of unborn souls. In the Zohar the treasure—house of unborn souls is located in the Garden of Eden, though it is sometimes identified with *Shekhinah*, who gives birth to the soul.[16]

> There are three parts to man's soul: *nefesh*, *ruah*, and *neshamah*. When he dies, his *nefesh* remains by the gravesite; his *ruah* (the 'spirit) goes to the terrestrial

Garden of Eden, and his *neshamah* ('soul') goes to the palaces in the celestial Garden of Eden.[17]

Ruah upon death enters the earthly Garden of Eden, where she assumes a shape resembling her earthly body. According to kabbalah, before descending to earth each soul is clothed in an ethereal body resembling the physical body she will inhabit on earth. She retrains this form while in the physical body until shortly before death, and then regains it afrerward. *Neshamah*, the highest level of soul, upon death, ascends to the heavenly Garden of Eden, the dwelling place of *Shekhinah*, whence *neshamah* issued into the world. Returning to her source, *neshamah* kindles the lamp of *Shekhinah*, who is encompassed by *neshamah* below and by the higher *sefirot* above.[18,19,20]

"Fine as frost on the ground" Exodus 16:4 is the flow of emanation likened to dew, trickled from *Keter* (known as the Holy Ancient One) to the configuration of *sefirot* surrounding *Tif'eret* (known as Short Tempered One). *Tif'eret* Himself is known as Heaven. The dew then descended further, finally congealing on earth as the manna . . . bread from heaven. The unique fragrance of manna derived from the Garden of Eden, through which it had passed on its journey down to earth. Miraculously, the manna tasted like whatever each one desired. Young men ate it like bread . . . the older people like a wafer in honey (Exodus 16:31) . . . the sucklings like milk from their mothers' breasts . . . the sick like porridge blended with honey. Afterward, they blessed G-d again by reciting the Grace after Meals, which Moses instituted for this occasion.[21]

By fasting one stimulates the *sefirotic* process according to the human pattern: liver, then heart, then brain. The person's own fat and blood, together with his intention are offered to *Shekhinah* (the liver) who offers it to *Tif'eret* (the heart) who offers it to *Hokhmah* and *Binah* (the brain) who rule over the entire *sefirotic* body. On a day of normal eating, the divine process unfolds in the reverse order.[22] "The body is commended because the spirit achieves its ascent through the commandments fulfilled by means of the body."[23]

The letter *'He'* is often a feminine marker, alluding to the Divine Mother, *Binah*, who nourishes Her offspring, the lower *sefirot*. Her flow, pictured as anointing oil, saturates *Yesod* (known as Righteous One), who pours into *Shekhinah*. "White from within red" refers to the respective tendencies of *Hesed* (characteristic of *Yesod)* and *Gevurah* (characteristic of *Shekhinah*). *Myrrh* is a reddish resin; *frankincense*, whitish. The full verse in Song of Songs reads: Before the day breathes and the shadows flee (i.e., the break of dawn), I will hasten to the mountain of *myrrh* and to the hill of *frankincense*.[24]

In this mysterious book are recorded various permutations of the name YHVH, according to different vowel combinations. The generated lights carry the Dwelling which symbolizes *Shekhinah*. Rabbi Yehudah the Prince states that he was once shown the Book of Adam, which contained the genealogy of the entire human race. The Zohar's Book of Adam is not to be confused with the Book of Adam in Apocrypha. According to various medieval tradtions, the angel Raziel transmitted a magical book to Adam. Later, probably in the seventeenth century, *Sefer Raziel* (the Book of Raziel) was compiled in its present form, comprising ancient magical, mystical, and cosmological teachings.[25]

Shekhinah is symbolized by the Ark, which contains the Covenant, symbolizing *Yesod*. This divine *aron*, ark is an appropriate container for the divine male body, the archetype of the human form. Correspondingly, pious humans are buried in an *aron*, a coffin.[26]

Slavery and Redemption

In the grace after meals the cup of blessing is used only if three have eaten together because the cup symbolizes

Shekhinah, who is blessed by the *sefirotic* triad of *Hesed*, *Gevurah*, and *Tiferet* (symbolized by the three patriarchs, Abraham, Isaac, and Jacob).

One takes the cup in both hands and gives it to the person saying the blessing who receives it in both hands moving it to the right hand since the blessing flows to *Shekhinah* primarily from *Hesed* on the right.[27]

> *Binah* is the voice of the divine shofar, from which issues the voice (or the sound), namely *Tiferet*, who is symbolized by Jacob. All three patriarchal *sefirot* (*Hesed*, *Gevurah*, and *Tiferet*) arose in *Hokhmah*, who is known as Thought, and they issued together from the shofar of *Binah*. Just as the voice (or sound) of a shofar is generated by moist, warm breath ('water, fire, and air as one') so the Divine Mother, *Binah*, generated all three patriarchal *sefirot* . . . *Hesed, Gevurah,* and *Tiferet* . . . who are symbolized respectively by water, fire and air. These three became "one in one voice," since *Tiferet* includes both *Hesed* and *Gevurah*, just as Jacob was the culmination of the patriarchs.[28]

The first five plagues in Egypt were delivered by the fingers of divine right hand (*Hesed*), whose gentle quality enabled

Pharaoh to still exercise his free will and decide on his own to harden his heart. Once this first round of plagues was completed, and Pharaoh did not repent, the last five plagues were delivered by the fingers of the left hand (*Gevurah*), whose harsh quality robbed Pharaoh of his independent will and hardened his heart automatically.[29]

The first of the Ten Commandments (I am YHVH your G-d) is parallel to the first utterance of Creation . . . Let there be light! Because G-d is light as indicated from a verse in Psalms. The second utterance of Creation is parallel to the second commandment 'You shall have no other gods . . . ' Israel is considered the firmament since they are linked to *Tif'eret* (known as Heaven) and they are joined to one true G-d. Other nations are entrusted to the heavenly princes and Israel is ruled directly by *Tif'eret,* who is called the firmament of heaven. The third commandment (You shall not take the name . . .) is parallel to the third utterance of Creation: Let the waters under the heaven be gathered. When one swears a false oath (taking G-d's name in vain) s/he separates *Shekhinah* (the Mother) from her partner, *Tif'eret*. All the *sefirot* crowns are disturbed (*Hesed* through *Yesod*). Mother also refers to Binah, who would be separated from Her sefirotic children and such an act diverts the flow from the site of divine union (the place of truth) to the demonic powers (another place, of falsehood).

The fourth commandment to remember the Sabbath day . . . parallels the fourth utterance of Creation . . . Let the earth sprout grass . . . because the earth symbolizes *Shekhinah* who is known as the Holy Land or earth. On the Sabbath She is arrayed in the lower *sefirotic* crowns. *Shekhinah* flourishes as She unites with *Tiferet* and sprouts grass (spreads life) and blessing below. To honor your mother and father (fifth commandment) parallels the fifth utterance of Creation . . . Let there be light in the firmament of heaven . . . because these lights symbolize the divine parents. Father *Tiferet* is symbolized by the sun and Mother *Shekhinah* is symbolized by the moon. He is known as the blessed Holy One and She is known as Assembly of Israel. The verses in Genesis and Exodus complement each other . . . "all is one." The sixth utterance of Creation "Let the waters swarm with a swarm of living beings" is parallel to the sixth commandment to not murder. The human being is a living being and humans should not devour each other as do the fish. The seventh commandment against committing adultery is parallel to the seventh utterance of Creation: "Let the earth bring forth beings after their kind." After their kind implies that a person should engender children only with his or her own mate. You shall not steal is parallel to the eighth utterance of Creation: "I have given you every seed-bearing plant." One who bears false witness is considered to have done so against G-d so the ninth commandment to not bear false witness against your fellow parallels the ninth utterance of Creation: "Let us make a human in our image." The tenth commandment to not covet your neighbor's wife . . . is parallel to the tenth utterance: "It is not good for the human to be alone; I will make him a helper alongside (or: corresponding to, as a counterpart to, opposite, facing) him." The parallel between the ten utterances and the Ten Commandments demonstrates that the world endures only for the sake and through the power, of Torah.[30]

Various supernatural phenomena were fashioned by G-d in the closing moments of the six days of Creation. Among these were three elements of the Ten Commandments: the tablets, the letters to be engraved on the tablets, and the unique engraving of the letters, which miraculously could be read from both the front and the back of the tablets.[31]

. . . Even *reiqanin*, the empty ones, among you (i.e., Israel) are as full of *mitsvot* as a pomegranate (is full of seeds)." The bells of gold (like on Aaron's robe) Exodus 28:33 are symbols of revelation and inspiration as in Samson when the Holy Spirit rested upon him, his hairs tingled like a bell (Vayiqra Rabbah 8:2).[32]

Shekhinah dwells at the site of the Holy of Holies, which lies at the center of the world, and even though the Temple has been destroyed and the Holy of Holies no longer exists, the entire world is still nourished for the sake of this central point and of G-d's Presence there. It is still fitting regardless of where one lives and prays to bless G-d for the good land He has given you, since the power and merit of the Land ensure sustenance for all.[33]

One of the miracles regularly performed in the Temple was that 'the wind never prevailed over the column of smoke. When the column of smoke went forth from the altar of the ascent offering, it rose straight up like a staff until it reached the sky. When the column of incense went forth from the golden altar, it entered straight into the chamber of the Holy of Holies. In the *Zohar*, whereas the smoke of most sacrifices ascends in a straight path to heaven, the smoke from nightly offerings ascends in a twisted way, finally reaching the haunt of evil spirits and nourishing them, thereby assuaging them so that they do not wreak havoc on earth. Here, the twisting smoke indicates its demonic nature.[34]

Eight things that correspond to the eight threads of the *zizit* (fringes), as it is written are the roots of critical percepts: "And remember all the commandments of the Lord." (Numbers 15:39) The first threads represents the eyes, that they should not see any sin; that man should not be haughty; that he should not go after his eyes; that he should not wink with his eyes. These are the negative percepts having to do with the eyes. Positive percepts are: "Only take heed to thyself, and keep thy soul diligently, lest thou forget that which thine eyes saw;" (Deuteronomy 4:9) "He will save him that is lowly of eyes;" (Job 22:29) "and for a memorial between thine eyes." (Exodus 13:9) The second thread represents the ears with a negative percept: "Thou shalt not hear a false report, not to listen to vain words." (Exodus 23:1) A positive precept is: "And now, O Israel, hearken unto the statutes." (Deuteronomy 4:1) The third thread represents the throat with a negative percept: "Thou shalt not eat any abominable thing." (Deuteronomy 14:3) A positive throat precept is to eat unleavened bread on Passover and so forth. The fourth thread represents the organs of speech, the mouth and the tongue, that these should not utter vain words, for if a man does this he transgresses a negative precept, as is written: "All things toil to weariness; man cannot utter it." (Ecclesiastes 1:8) "Thou shalt not take the name of the Lord thy G-d in vain." (Exodus 20:7) "And ye shall not swear by My name falsely." (Leviticus 19:12) "Nor lie to one another." (Leviticus 19:11) "Thou shalt not bear false witness." (Exodus 20:13) Positive precepts of the mouth and tongue are: "And thou shalt teach them diligently unto thy children." (Deuteronomy 6:7) "And my tongue shall speak of Thy righteousness." (Psalms 35:28) The fifth thread represents the hands with two negative percepts: "Put not thy hand with the wicked." (Exodus 23:1) "Thou shalt not rob." (Leviticus 19:13) Positive precepts are: "Thou shalt surely open thy hand." (Deuteronomy 15:8) "And thou shall bind them for a sign upon thy hand." (Deuteronomy 6:8) The sixth thread represents the feet with these negative percepts: "Thou shalt not go up and down as a talebearer." (Leviticus 19:16) "And go not after other gods." (Jeremiah 25:6) "And he that hasteth with his feet sinneth." (Proverbs 19:2) Positive precepts of the feet are: "After the Lord your G-d shall ye walk." (Deuteronomy 13:5) "Ye shall walk in all the way which the Lord your G-d hath commanded you." (Deuteronomy 5:30) "Guard thy foot when thou goest to the house of G-d." (Ecclesiastics 4:17) The seventh thread corresponds to the sexual organ with negative and positive percepts: "Thou shalt not commit adultery." (Exodus 20:13) "And you, be ye fruitful, and multiply." (Genesis 9:7) The eighth thread corresponds to the nose with a negative percept containing anger, stubbornness, and smelling the perfumes of idols: "And there shall cleave nought of the devoted thing to thy hand." (Deuteronomy 13:17) The positive precept is to smell myrtle branches on the Sabbath and so forth. (Deuteronomy 13:18)

All humankind is encouraged to remember these eight things allowing them to always be in our hearts. One, the eyes: two, the ears; three, the tongue; four, the throat; five, the hands; six, the feet; seven, the sexual organ; eight, the nose. We are commanded to not sin with any of these things and our hearts should be on each to plan how to keep His commandments.[35]

Kabbalists rise at midnight to study Torah and stimulate the union of the *sefirot* symbolized by the letters YHVH. By devoted study they cleave to *Shekhinah*. In Psalms 119:62 it is written that a harp suspended above King David's bed would play by itself at midnight by a wind from the north and David would arise and study Torah until dawn. In the Zohar the midnight ritual is expanded saying G-d delights in the souls of the righteous in the Garden of Eden, and those who study Torah below partake in the joy.[36] By arising at midnight kabbalists adorn Shekhinah with words of Torah in preparation for Her union with King *Tiferet*. Others unite with their spouses in holiness on the midnight of Shabbat, the sacred moment of the coupling at the wedding of the divine couple whose union they imitate and to whom they cleave. The Mishnah (Ketubbot 5:6) discusses how often husbands are required to fulfill *Onah* (conjugal rights): those who are unoccupied . . . every day; laborers twice a week; donkey-drivers, once a week; camel-drivers, once every thirty days; sailors once every six months.[37]

At each end of the ark's gold cover a cherub was hammered out and the two cherubim faced each other, with their heads bent slightly downward and their fully outstretched wings turned upward. The divine voice was thought to issue from the space above the gold cover (*kapporet*) and between the two cherubim. The Babylonian Talmud (BT Bava Batra 99a) discusses the cherubim in Solomon's Temple as miraculously moving their wings up and down three times each day at prayer time.[38] Rabbi Yeisa posed a riddle regarding the transition from primordial unity to multiplicity. A *sefirotic* solution is a primordial egg issuing from the divine bird, splits into four. Two (*Hokhmah* and *Binah*) ascend, one (*Tif'eret*) descends, and one (*Yesod*) spreads a flow into the sea of *Shekhinah* or *Shekhinah* sprawls over the ocean of the world. A cosmic egg figures prominently in Orphic myth which has various affinities with the Zohar. The Orphic myth involves a primal serpent producing a cosmic egg and this serpent may be related to the uroboros (the serpent biting its tail), symbolizing an eternal cycle or the unity and renewal of life. The description of a "bird abiding in fire" probably refers to the phoenix, who like the uroboros symbolizes rebirth, immortality, and renewal. The mythological phoenix dies in a self-created fire every five-hundred-to-over-one-thousand years and burns into a pile of ashes, out of which a phoenix chick is born.[39]

ANGELS

According to the Babylonian Talmud (BT Sanhedrin 38b) *Hashem* created a company of administering angels and asked them if He should make a human being in our image? They questioned *Hashem* and He stretched out his little finger among them and burned them. He did the same with a second group. The third group assured He could do whatever he pleased. After the Flood and the Tower of Babel, the angels asked if the first groups of angels spoke well. He said: "Till your old age, I am He; till you turn gray, I will carry you, I have made and I will bear; I will carry and deliver. (Isaiah 46:4)[1] According to rabbinic tradition, the seventy nations of the world are governed by seventy angels or heavenly princes appointed by G-d. (Daniel 10:20, Genesis 9:19, Zohar 1:46b)[2] According to rabbinic tradition when the Torah was about to be revealed on Sinai ministering angels objected contending G-d's splendor should remain in or above the heavens and not be given to human beings on earth. G-d demonstrated to the angels that the Torah is intended for mortals who are vulnerable to sin and who need laws and regulations. The angels were convinced that the Torah is inappropriate for heavenly creatures.[3] According to various medieval traditions the angel Raziel transmitted a magical book to Adam, though after his departure from the Garden. The book preserves the primordial wisdom of paradise for Adam and his generations. Later (probably in the 17th century) *Sefer Razi'el* was compiled in its present form, comprising ancient magical, mystical, and cosmological teachings. Rabbi Yehudah the Prince was said to have once seen the book which contained the genealogy of the entire human race.[4]

The three archangels Michael, Gabriel, and Raphael are associated respectively with water, fire, and air. By drinking from a cup of wine at the conclusion of the blessing after meals, one stimulates a flow of blessing from above.[5] The four heads, or cardinal points, stemming from *Shekhinah* are each overseen by one of the four archangels: Michael (south), Gabriel (north), Raphael (west), and Uriel (east), each accompanied by two subordinate angels. Jacob's placement of his twelve-stone pillow corresponded precisely to the stations of these angels.[6]

The phrase 'two birds' refers to the two angels who dwell in *Shekhinah*. She is known as the Tree of Knowledge of Good and Evil, comprising life and death. In prophetic literature the 'Day of YHVH' is the day on which G-d will eventually reveal Himself to the nations in all His power and destroy Israel's enemies. It also refers to the final day of each person's life, when his/her soul returns to its divine source. The final blessing of the sitting prayer concludes: "Blessed are You, YHVH, who has redeemed Israel." There should be no pause between this blessing and the beginning of the *Amidah*, the standing prayer—*Shekhinah* is adorned during the sitting prayer in preparation for Her union with *Tiferet*, which takes place during the *Amidah*.[7]

"Enoch walked with G-d, and he was no more, for G-d took him." The radiance within Enoch's body was to be revealed in heaven in the form of Metatron. Genesis (5:24) This embarrassed the angels who had opposed the creation of human beings since here was a human so virtuous that he was transformed into the head angel. Metatron is often described as *na'ar* (youth, lad, servant, deputy). Rabbi Shim'on alludes to the identification of Enoch with Metatron by citing the statement from Proverbs, "Train the youth" which is understood to mean that *Hanokh* (Enoch) was transformed into Metatron (youth). The chief angel is continually rejuvenated (by the radiance 'constantly inside him') and he carries out divine mission throughout the worlds. In time of

Judgment, he assuages divine wrath.[8] The angel Metatron is closely linked with *Shekhinah*, who is also known as *Elohim* (whereas YHVH designates *Tif'eret*). Enoch surrendered his earthly name when he was transformed into Metatron, a heavenly name associated with *Elohim* (or *Shekhinah*).[9] The ascent of Enoch is also considered to be a humiliation for the angels.[10]

G-d delights each night with the souls of the righteous in the Garden of Eden, and both He and they listen to those who rise at midnight to study Torah. *Shekhinah*, the Foundation Stone, is also known as 'precious stone' and She is surrounded by twelve angels, symbolized by the twelve precious stones arranged in four rows in the breastplate of the high priest.[11] In the breastplate of the high priest, twelve precious stones were arranged in four rows; each stone was engraved with a name of one of the twelve tribes, who in the wilderness each camped in one of the four directions. In the Zohar these twelve stones also symbolize twelve angels surrounding *Shekhinah* in all four directions. She is arrayed above by angels and below by the twelve tribes. The hours of the day correspond to *Tif'eret*, the hours of the night to *Shekhinah*. During the three watches of the night, angels serve and sing, while beneath them stand countless forces who receive sustenance from *Shekhinah*. Midnight falls in the middle of the second four-hour watch of the night. Here two rows of angels correspond to the two hours preceding midnight, and two other rows to the two hours following midnight. The rows of angels are symbolized by the rows of stone in Exodus 28:17.[12]

The image of 'twelve oxen beneath the sea' refers to a large bronze reservoir built by King Solomon in the Temple, which rested on twelve bronze oxen, three facing outward in each direction. The sea symbolizes *Shekhinah*; the twelve oxen Her accompanying angels.[13] The Messiah will judge humanity by his sense of smell, heightened by awe of YHVH. Only Moses, Solomon, and the Messiah judge(d) the world without formal legal procedures. Each myriad of angelic camps (Uriel, Michael, Gabriel, and Raphael) has one of the 365 keys of light, opening channels by which the supernal light flows down from above.[14]

Israel's failure stimulated war and the dimming of *Shekhinah*. The Second Temple (symbolizing Her) was destroyed by Rome (known as Edom), and She went into exile along with her angels (known as the twelve tribes) and their camps (lower angels or the tribes of Israel). Each of the twelve tribes represents 100 years. The ten tribes of the northern kingdom of Israel (exiled by the Assyrians in 721 BCE) symbolize 1,000 years; the two tribes Judah and Benjamin (exiled by the Babylonians in 586 BCE) symbolize 200 years.[15] If the Israelites had not sinned by worshiping the Golden Calf and causing Moses to smash the tablets, the history of the world would have been entirely different and Israel's future would not have been tainted by suffering and exile. Rather, they would have been angelic beings.[16] The angelic camps who adore *Shekhinah* are called to present themselves. The presiding angel appears, holding four keys, which unlock the treasures of emanation for the lower worlds. Each of these keys is engraved with one letter of the name YHVH. The first three keys turn into one, and the fourth key then joins with this one composite key. By bringing these two keys into the Garden, the angels stimulate the union of the divine couple, corresponding to Israel's act of unification (by reciting the *Shema*) below.[17]

Two fallen angels (Uzza and Aza'el) opposed the creation of Adam and Eve, fell from heaven, were attracted by the daughters of humankind, and inherited dust. These two angels are identified with the two spies sent by Joshua to Jericho, apparently based on the image of angels spying on human beings. The human daughters are seen as demonic figures and identified with the two prostitutes who approached King Solomon, each claiming to be the mother of the same infant. Solomon's wisdom enabled him to overwhelm these demonic forces, who previously could not be vanquished.[18] Uzza and Aza'el were cast down into the world as *Nefilim* (sons of G-d); they persuaded men to go whoring and after idolatrous practices. As a result of their sin they were removed to the mountains of darkness and chained there. Uzza and Aza'el asked to go down and sanctify the name of G-d but were overcome with the evil inclination and could not control it.[19]

In *Dumah* (literally meaning silence and the name for the netherworld) the angel in charge of the souls of the dead deals with the soul. The corpse is punished by *hibbut ha-quever* (beating in the grave) by the Angel of Death or other heavenly or demonic beings. Most souls are punished in Hell and eventually purified of their sins. After ascending from Hell the soul is bathed and perfumed, and finally offered as a sacrifice by the heavenly angel and priest Michael.[20]

In 2 Kings (2:11) Elijah ascended in a whirlwind to heaven without dying whereas all other human beings must die before their souls can ascend. Elijah became an angel like the other angels and like those who cleave most to the King . . . namely other select souls. In Malachi (3:23-24) Elijah is associated with the Messianic age and in the Babylonian Talmud (BT Bava Batra 121b) he is described as "still existing."[21]

The garments in which the priest is clothed are all within the supernal mystery, in that the garments below are modeled on the garments above. Michael is the High Priest and comes from the right side.[22]

The Tripartite Soul consists of *nefesh, ruah,* and *neshamah.* They are joined to one another like the links of a chain and they work together. The lowest part, *nefesh* receives illumination and sustenance from the *ruah*; the *ruah* is illumined and sustained by the *neshamah*, which receives light and influence from the upper worlds. The *nefesh* is attached to the body, preserving it and satisfying its needs. The body depends upon it and it depends upon the body. The *nefesh* has no light of its own at all. It is the instinctive power of feeling and action needed to sustain the body. The *ruah* is an intermediate power whose task is to illumine the *nefesh*; it is often referred to as the throne of the *nehamah* or the luminary of the *nefesh*. The *neshamah* allows man to study Torah and obey the commandments. Besides practical religious and daily practice it allows perception of divine mystery. It is the spark of the Divine. He breathed into his nostrils the breath (*neshamah*) of life: it is the spiritual-religious force that draws man near to G-d and preserves the bonds between them. This is the meaning of: "I have created him for My glory: for the sake of my glory, so that he might restore it with powerful pillars, and beautify it with improvement and adornment from below, so that My glory might be exalted through the merit of the righteous in the earth." (Isaiah 43:7)[23]

> *Hesed (Love)* and *Din* (Judgment) are combined and unified . . . the left intertwined with the right. Fire becomes incorporated in water and water in fire. The red of fire and blood acts in conjunction with the white of smoke that rises from the alter. The isolation of any attribute upsets the balance of forces within the G-dhead. *Din* is tempered by and becomes subject to the rule of *Hesed*. The wood laid on the alter mollifies the furious powers of the fires of *Din*. The fire is swallowed up in the smoke and *Din* is sweetened by the sweet savor. The union of *Tiferet* and *Malkhut* is likened to the union of the sun and moon; the binding together of the oral and written Torah; the relationship of Boaz and Ruth. *Shekhinah* compares herself to incense and her husband to oil, and ergo the burning of incense with oil affects intercourse.[24]

> The High Priest stands for Michael, who ministers in the Tabernacle of Metatron, and his garments, which are patterned on those of supernal glory, are described as if they were like the garments of Michael, which are formed from a mixture of the lights that shine in the *Shekhinah*. The breastplate and the ephod,

as well as the *Urim* and *Tummim*, represent *Tiferet* and *Malkhut*, and the rings that join the breastplate and the ephod together are formed through the mystery of the *Ofannim* and the *Hayyot*, which assist *Shekhinah* to achieve intercourse. Therefore when the priest puts these clothes on he is like the supernal image. The stones in the breastplate and the ephod testify to the High Priest's righteousness or his wickedness, while with the gold plate on his forehead the High Priest is able to tell whether the person he is facing is righteous or wicked. Even the most hardened sinners are moved to contrition when they look upon this gold plate, and if they go on to repent their sins are forgiven.[25]

Dreams come in many levels and they are all part of the mystery of Wisdom. Dream is one level, and vision is one level, and prophecy is one level, and they are all levels one above the other.[26]

The holy Rabbi Ze'ev of Zbarazh expounds the verse: 'And the angel of the Lord appeared unto him in a flame of fire out of the midst of a bush . . . but the bush was not consumed.' (Exodus 3:2) Even though the bush was not consumed and was still full of evil character traits yet the Lord appears there if there is 'a flame of fire,' namely, yearning and longing. My brother, if you will reflect on these words you will discover in this parable counsels and paths and encouragements for the worship of G-d.

All this only applies when man digs deep into the recesses of his heart in order to recognize Him at whose word the world came into being. But if he makes not the slightest effort to search for it, then: 'The fool walketh in darkness' (Ecclesiastes 2:14) and 'A fool hath no delight in understanding.' (Proverbs 18:2) That is to say, in repentance from the depth of his heart. And he then knows nothing of how remote he is from the L-rd. He imagines he is near and that he knows all.[27]

CIRCUMCISION, SOULS, REINCARNATION, AND RESURRECTION

Circumcision

In the ritual of circumcision, first the foreskin is cut and removed, disclosing the mucous membrane, which is torn down the center and pulled back, revealing the corona. The act of tearing and pulling back the membrane is called *Peri'ah*, uncovering the corona. "If one circumcises but does not uncover the circumcision, it is as if he has not circumcised." (Moses de Leon, *Sheqel ha-Qodesh*, 55 (67)) Through the double ritual of circumcision, one overcomes the two monsters, the demonic couple Samael and Lilith.[1]

"I have set my bow in the cloud." (Genesis 1:9) This is *Hashem*'s declaration to Noah after the flood, giving the divine covenant with humanity . . . the rainbow. The bow often represents the divine phallus and the site of the covenant (the sign of circumcision).[2]

Through the act of circumcision, one enters the sefirotic realm of *Yesod*, the divine phallus. *Yesod* is known as Righteous One, based on Proverbs 10:25. The Righteous One is an everlasting foundation or the Righteous One is the foundation of the world. Abraham was originally Avram and was changed to Avraham in Genesis 17:5 because through the act of circumcision he attained intimacy with *Shekhinah*, who is symbolized by the second *he* of the divine name YHVH. Then this letter is added to his name, transforming Avram into Avraham.[3]

The *olah* (ascent offering) ascending to the *sefirot* above *Shekhinah* must be male. The offerings must be *tamim* meaning blameless, complete, intact, free of blemish, impeccable, perfect. When Abraham was 99 years old YHVH appeared and told him to walk in His presence and be complete (*tamim*) and He will grant His covenant between Me and you and I will increase you very greatly. This divine directive is soon followed by the covenantal command of circumcision. (Genesis 17:1-2) Through this ritual, a man becomes *tamim*, complete or unblemished; without circumcision, paradoxically, a man is blemished. (Genesis 17: 9-14)[4]

Man becomes a 'son' to G-d when he reaches the age of 13 . . . from then on he becomes liable to punishment from Heaven for his misdeeds. Before the age of 13, the *neshamah*, the celestial and holiest part of the soul, does not settle upon man, and he is under domination of the evil inclination, which derives from 'the other side,' called 'uncircumcision.'[5]

> As Israel was about to be liberated from Egyptian bondage, G-d wished to unite with them; but the demonic power (symbolized by foreskin) still covered the divine light. G-d commanded the male Israelites to circumcise themselves (removing the foreskin) and to consume the Passover sacrifice quickly. Meanwhile, Satan occupied himself with Job, 'taking what was his' and no longer interfering in Israel's offering to G-d nor impeding the union between G-d and Israel.[6]

The Soul, Reincarnation, and Resurrection

"He fashioned everything at its appropriate time." (Ecclesiastes 3:11) From this comes the notion that One kept creating worlds and destroying them until he created these (heaven and earth). This is what inspired Isaac Luria's theory of the breaking of the vessels. Primordial matter is formless, despite transient appearances.[7]

Moses died on Sabbath afternoon during the time of Divine favor, and his soul was treasured away in the Divine Will.[8] If one's apparent virtue on earth was genuine and sincere it will determine if his soul needs reincarnation.[9] The souls of children issue on Sabbath eve from *Tif'eret*, who is known as truth, Jacob, and the blessed Holy One.[10] By fulfilling a commandment, a person strengthens the corresponding *sefirotic* limb; by transgressing a commandment, one impairs the corresponding limb and consequently his misdeed is exposed by that *sefirah*.[11] In the Book of Daniel (4:32): "All the inhabitants of earth are considered as nothing. He does as He wishes with the host of heaven and the inhabitants of earth. There is no one who can stay His hand or say to Him, 'What have You done?'"[12]

According to the Bible (2 Kings 11:12), the prophet Elijah did not die a normal death but was carried off to heaven in a chariot of fire. He became associated with the Messianic age (Malachi 3:23-24) and in rabbinic tradition is described as 'still existing (BT Bava Batra 121b) and revealing divine secrets to righteous humans.' (BT Bava Metsi'a 59b, BT Mishnah Sotah 9:15) attributes to Rabbi Pinhas the following teaching: "Zeal leads to cleanliness, cleanliness leads to purity, purity leads to restraint, restraint leads to holiness, holiness leads to humility, humility leads to fear of sin, fear of sin leads to *hasidut* (love, devotion), *hasidut* leads to Holy Spirit, Holy Spirit leads to resurrection of the dead, and resurrection of the dead comes through Elijah, remembered for good."[13]

The tribe of Ephraim miscalculated the divinely decreed length of the Egyptian bondage and made a premature exodus; they were punished, nearly all of them being killed by the Philistines. Eventually their dry bones were resurrected by Ezekiel. G-d's words to the prophet indicate that Ephraim is called Israel: "these bones are the whole house of Israel." Because Ephraim epitomized all of Israel, Jacob favored him over his older brother Manasseh with the blessing of the firstborn. Consequently, in the wilderness of Sinai the tribe of Ephraim journeyed on the west, symbolizing *Shekhinah*, who is known as Assembly of Israel.[14]

"While the body is from the female, it is the soul that is from the male, for the soul is the substance of a particular body." The "endurance to rise" may allude to an almond, a bone supposed to be at the base of the spine, shaped like an almond, and indestructible—and from which G-d will one day resurrect decomposed bodies. Those who attained burial in the land of Israel will rouse first.[15] It is said in Ecclesiastes (4:2-3) "I praise the dead, who have already died, more than the living, who are still alive. But better than both is one who has not yet been, who has not seen the evil deeds that are being done under the sun." "The dead, who have already died" refers to those who died in a previous lifetime and were then reincarnated and enabled to fulfill their souls before dying again.[16]

Yesod is called peace because He creates harmony by uniting *Tiferet* with *Shekhinah*. The four directions (east, west, south, and north) are linked with the four elements (water, fire, air, and earth or dust) which often symbolize the four *sefirot*: *Hesed, Gevurah, Tiferet,* and *Shekhinah*. The human being is a microcosm, including aspects of the entire world and modeled on the sefirotic structure ('designed . . . in His array').[17]

Rabbi Elie Kaplan Spitz provides an excellent overview of the dying process, death, and reincarnation in his book, *Does the Soul Survive? A Jewish Journey to Belief in Afterlife, Past Lives* and *Living with Purpose*.

1. The Dying Process

> Rav Nahman appearing in a dream, soon after his death, to his friend Raba; Rav Nahman described the moment of death as like 'pulling a hair out of milk.'[18]

As the soul leaves the body it is met by a radiant light, which is termed *Shekhinah*, or divine-feminine presence, in mystical writings. Hence, the Zohar explains, 'When a man is on the point of leaving this world . . . the *Shekhinah* shows herself to him, and then the soul goes out in joy and love to meet the *Shekhinah*. If he is righteous, he cleaves and attaches himself to her. But if not, then the *Shekhinah* departs, and the soul is left behind, mourning for its separation from the body.'

Just as the biblical patriarchs were 'gathered to their people,' so the Zohar describes, 'At the hour of a man's departure from the world, his father and his relatives gather around him . . . and they accompany his soul to the place where it is to abide.' But before the soul can move, the individual must look back to review his or her life. The Talmud records: 'When a man departs to review his eternal home all his deeds are enumerated before him and he is told: Such and such a thing have you done, in such and such a place on that day.'[19]

2. Separation from the Physical Body

In the Jerusalem Talmud Rabbi Levi says the soul hovers over the dead body for three days hoping to return and departing only when there is no more hope of return. The Zohar states that for seven days the soul (*nefesh*) goes to and from the grave and the house mourning for the body.

3. Emotional Purification

The torments of *Gehenna* (hell) are a state of mind not a place. Upon death there is an intense encounter with unresolved negative emotions (dark and dishonorable). The encounter enables the cleansing through abreaction, discharge, and catharsis of the *ruach*.

4. Final Completion of the Personality

Once the soul is cleansed of the negative emotion it undergoes two transformations. It experiences emotional bliss and the accumulated learning of the *ruach* is passed onto the *neshamah*, the higher self that provides insight that completes the personality. This is the journey through the lower levels of *Gan Eden*. The postmortem being enters into the world of the infinite, the Divine. It is G-d's original earthly creation and its corresponding ethereal mirror.

5. Heavenly Repose of the Soul

The *neshamah* dips into the River of Light and has another life review, from the perspective of many lifetimes. From the perspective of the eternal transpersonal self . . . the most recent life becomes apparent. The *Gan Eden* experience is dependent on the level of consciousness achieved in this life. Further evolution occurs in this realm for movement in the "seven heavens." The *neshamah's* repose is completed and it begins another transit stage.

6. Return to the Source

In *Gan Eden* the highest levels of the soul (*chayah* or *yechidah*) which are direct extensions of G-d are unfettered by the soul's lower levels and are able to experience the joy of G-d's presence. The lower levels of the soul return to their source (*tzror hachayim*) the storehouse of life where it receives its message for the next reincarnation (*gilgulei neshamot*) that translates to 'the rolling of the souls' from body to body.[20]

7. Preparation for Rebirth

A medieval text *Seder Yetzirat Ha-Vlad* (the Creation of the Embryo) gives the image of a life preview as a preparation for rebirth: Between morning and evening the angel carries the soul around and shows him/her where s/he will live and where s/he will die, and the place where s/he will be buried, and s/he takes him/her through the whole world, and points out the just and the sinners and all things. In the evening s/he replaces him/her in the womb of the mother, and there s/he remains for nine months . . . Finally, the time comes for the soul to enter the world. It is reluctant to leave; but the angel touches the baby on the nose, extinguishes the light above the head, and sends it forth into the world. Instantly, the soul forgets all that it has seen and learned and enters the world, crying, having just lost a place of shelter, rest, and security.[21]

Nahmanides (Spain-Israel 1194-1270) believed that the final reward entails reunification of soul and body. In this re-embodied state humanity will endure eternally. In the Messianic Era (*olam baba*) or the world to come the body will not necessarily need food or water. We will bask in G-d's light like Moshe did for forty days and nights. Our united body and soul is a microcosm of the universe and an essential part of G-d's plan.[22]

Isaac Luria (b 1569 CE Safed Israel) believed that a person's soul is composed of a package of soul sparks originating with Adam and passed down over the generations. Our goal in life is to elevate our soul sparks in order to heal a fallen Adam which will enable cosmic, messianic harmony. Luria believed creation was a four-act drama directed by *Hashem*:

Act I *Ein Sof* (infinity): G-d who is infinite, filled all.

Act II *Tzimtzum* (contraction): G-d withdrew inwardly to create a sphere of emptiness into which G-d could craft creation. G-d finished vessels in the void into which G-d emanated a divine ray of light.

Act III *Shevirat HaKelim* (the shattering of the vessels): The divine light was too powerful and the vessels exploded; a product of G-d's plan. Holy sparks flew in all directions and were dispersed among the broken shards; the Big Bang theory in physics.

Act IV *Tikkum* (repair): G-d reconstituted enough of the broken shards to enable people to help G-d continue the repair. Human beings would be given the capacity, free will, and duty to help gather the holy sparks. Such extraction of sparks from the shards would be achieved by the doing of G-d's decrees (*mitzvoth*) with proper intention (*kavannah*). By eating the forbidden fruit Adam fell several spiritual levels and some of the sparks were displaced more deeply into Adam's body. All humans begin life with soul sparks originating with Adam.[23]

A fuller description of Luria's vision of creation:

G-d wished to allow for the potential of finitude to be expressed, that returns in process to infinity. Initially the sphere G-d evacuated is an impression of previous infinite light and emptiness. G-d enters emptiness from the top (half-way) to the center forming concentric circles of *sefirot* (divine attributes). The *sefirot* take the form of pillars which constitute *Adam Kadmon* the primordial human which is the root of the vessels themselves. *Adam Kadmon* is in the realm above the highest spiritual levels of the world known as *Atzilut*. All on the level of divine self-creation is perfect.

In a complex process of the lights return to the infinite and back again to the finite they become differentiated and vessels begin to form. G-d brings the lower levels to the upper levels of *Adam kadmon* and emanates ten vessels of light back to the lower levels. Three light vessels in the highest sphere represent the levels of transcendence, will, and intelligence and contain the re-emanated light. The seven lower vessels, fashioned in an unbalanced way, shatter. The lights return above, and the vessels descend to the levels that will later become the lower worlds. Then G-d emanates a 'new face' that is balanced, and this divine emanation begins to reconstitute the fallen sparks.

To re-create the divine realm of *yetzirah, Adam kadmon* mates internally, thereby allowing for a reconstituted world (*olam hatikkum*). *Adam Kadmon* still consists of ten *sefirot* now organized into five faces (*partzufim*) composed of five main *sefirot: Keter; Chochmah; Binah* (that face each other). *Tiferet* and *Malkhut* which below were back-to-back are raised by *Keter* to return face-to-face. Adam of the Torah is *Adam HaRishon* formed through the merger of *Binah* and *Tiferet* as they rise up to *Keter* and *Chokhman. Adam HaRishon* was supposed to return to *Malkhut* and *Tiferet* face-to-face on the lower level, so as to make an uninterrupted chain of *tikkum* from *Ein Sof* to the lower levels.

After eating the forbidden fruit *Adam HaRishon* falls into the physical world (*Olam haAssiya*) . . . a lower spiritual plane. Sparks scatter in all directions because *Olam haAssiyah* is filled with profane shards (*kelipot*) from the breaking of the vessels. Some of the sparks are thrust deeper within *Adam haRishon* which he passes on to this descendents. Other sparks fall among the *kelipot*, a scattering that leaves *Adam haRishon* and G-d, the source of the sparks, incomplete.

Family members are rarely from the same soul root allowing complementary cooperation in a family because souls un-rectified from the same root are in competition for the same scarce resources in the shattered world. This is analogous to different personality types in astrology that can complement each other by their differences and clash when the same types are brought together. Souls of the same root are able to use intentionality to rise higher and gain by combining forces. When the soul spark is purified by acts of intentionality the spark may rise, enabling a reunification and healing of *Adam haRishon*.[24]

The early mystics and among the Hasidim it is specified that in earlier lives the person lived as a Jew, usually of the same sex. There are exceptions to this rule with some accounts of Jews having lived as non-Jews in the past and of the opposite gender, but these are exceptions to the rule.[25]

Rabbi Kaplan Spitz provides an image to conceptualize how to better nurture the soul:

> Imagine soul as a hollow, glasslike bead, composed of light, at the center of our being. The bead has three colored bands nestled one on top of the other, kind of like the concentric circles of color on a jawbreaker candy. Spirit flows through the center of the bead. It is warm, sweet light that passes through the bead in all directions. This spirit emerges from the Divine.
>
> The three bands of the bead, from the outer to the inner, represent the physical, emotional, and intellectual dimensions of our life. The degree of transparency of these beads is ever-changing, reflecting in auralike ways our accumulated experiences. We are born with this hollow three-banded, vessel-like bead, in which are imbedded the memories of previous lives. When we die, this glasslike bead, composed of light, rises into an ethereal realm, in most cases destined to return into a new body. The divine spirit, which flows through the bead, remains unchanged, always flowing. The divine light flows to all parts of our

person, emerging through the bead, as if through a prism.

Our goal is to purify the three bands of color. The more transparent the glass, the greater is the flow of light from the center. Lines of discoloration or foggy patches form in varying degrees corresponding to the severity of injury that has occurred, whether by harm that has befallen us or harm we have caused to others. Scars are manifest as dark lines through which light can barely pass. When light from the spirit passes through the bead, it may resolve discolorations on the bands. Simultaneously, our deeds impact on the color and transparency, too. Acts of mindfulness and compassion can dissolve some of the discoloration. True healing is a joint product of our own efforts (will) and the light from within (grace).

The center of the bead is often clogged as if by sediment that builds from anxiety, selfishness, anger, fear, violence, and apathy. To cleanse the obscuring buildup requires an awareness of our past injuries and our current dysfunctional reflexes. There is a part of us (somehow removed form the elements of the bead) that allows us to examine the bead.[26]

To affirm and assist others includes an enthusiasm for celebrating life-cycle events with friends and family and marking communal anniversaries of key historical events. To become a vessel unified and illuminated by the light of spirit we must engage in acts of compassion and joy.

Our life's homework assignment is soul work. We have the opportunity to live with increasing awareness and generosity without any shortcuts. When we bring our entire person to the act, every act is potentially soulful. Sex can be just a physical release but with emotional commitment and spirit it can be an act of love, an intertwining of lives, and a touch of 'oneness.' When we access all dimensions of our being our lives are lived more fully with all facets of our soul engaged. We are drawn closer to G-d, the source of our spirit whenever our attention is focused in the present moment.[27]

> To enter and experience higher dimensions, the soul is enveloped in a radiant garment woven out of the good deeds performed by that person in this world (parallels appear in Islamic and Iranian eschatology and Mahayana Buddhism). 'Rabbi Abba states that the angels clothe the soul in her individual garment, which corresponds to *deyoqna*, the image, of this world.' This last phrase associates the soul's garment

with the *tselem*, image, an ethereal body. Before entering a human body, each soul exists in the Garden of Eden, where s/he is clothed in this *tselem*, which resembles the physical body s/he will inhabit on earth.[28]

H-olam ha-ba is the world that is coming. The term is often been understood as referring to the hereafter and often been translated as 'the world to come.' The world that is coming already exists, occupying another dimension. The wise call it *ha-olam ha-ba* not because it does not exist now, but for us today in this world it is still to come. 'The world to come' does not succeed this world in time, but exists from eternity as a reality outside and above time, to which the soul ascends. In kabbalah the 'world that is coming' often refers to *Binah*, the continuous source of emanation.[29]

When the time comes for the dead to be resurrected, the demonic Serpent will deliver bodies from their graves. This will happen toward the end of the sixth millennium . . . which is premature for a snake, whose normal period of gestation is seven years (or here, millennia), not six.[30]

G-d rewards the wicked in this world for whatever little good they may have done, in order to deprive them of eternal life in the world-to-come. The righteous on the other hand, are punished now for their few failings, in order to be fully rewarded in the hereafter.[31]

"The soul is originally androgynous, reflecting the nature of both its divine parents, *Tif'eret* and *Shekhniah*. Afterward, it splits in two and each half manifests as one gender within either a male or a female body. If a man is worthy, he finds his original soul mate and they reunite."[32] Prior to departing from this life the soul and the body are both punished for being jointly responsible for misdeeds. At the moment of death the person sees *Shekhinah* and the soul departs from the body to reunite with Her.[33]

All three aspects of the soul are holy (*nefesh, ruah,* and *neshamah*) and derive and correspond to a particular *sefirah*. *Nefesh* derives from *Shekhinah*, *ruah* from *Tif'eret*, and *neshamah* from *Binah*. The three aspects or rungs of soul are arranged from lowest to highest. *Nefesh* is possessed by all people and animates us. *Ruah* stimulates one to explore G-d's ways and if proven worthy attains the highest rung of *neshamah*.[34]

Tamar learned in Judah's home the mysterious ways in which G-d conducts the world via the mysteries of reincarnation. The Zohar reveals that if a married man dies childless, his soul rolls restlessly through the world . . . unless his brother redeems his spirit through performing levirate marriage: marrying the widowed wife, impregnating her, and consciously drawing that homeless soul into the embryo. Reincarnation provides the spirit with another opportunity to engender new life. Tamar insured the reincarnation of the souls of Judah's childless sons Er and Onan by seducing Judah and bearing twins; Perez and Zerah, who were actually reincarnations of their uncles, Er and Onan.[35]

CONCLUDING THOUGHTS

As we become transparent, revealed for exactly who we are and not who we wish to be, then the mystery of human life as a whole glistens momentarily in a flash of incarnation. Spirituality emanates from the ordinariness of this human life made transparent by lifelong tending to its nature and fate.

The path of the soul will not allow concealment of the shadow without unfortunate consequences. You don't achieve the goal of the philosophers' stone, the lapis lazuli at the core of your heart, without letting all of human passion into the fray. It takes a lot of material, alchemically, to produce the refinement of the peacock's tail or the treasured gold—other images of the goal. But if you can tolerate the full weight of human possibility as the raw material for an alchemical, soulful life, then at the end of the path you may have a vision within yourself of the lapis and sense the stone idols of Easter Island standing nobly in your soul and the dolmen of Stonehenge marking eons of time in your own lifespan. Then your soul, cared for in courage, will be so solid, so weathered and mysterious, that divinity will emanate from your very being. You will have the spiritual radiance of the holy fool who has dared to live life as it presents itself and to unfold personality with its heavy yet creative dose of imperfection.

Spiritual life does not truly advance by being separated either from the soul or from its intimacy with G-d, as well as man, is fulfilled when G-d humbles himself to take on human flesh. The theological doctrine of incarnation suggests that G-d validates human imperfection as having mysterious validity and value. Our depressions, jealousies, narcissism, and failures are not at odds with the spiritual life. Indeed, they are essential to it. When tended, they prevent the spirit from zooming off into the ozone of perfectionism and spiritual pride. More important, they provide their own seeds of spiritual sensibility, which complement those that fall from the stars. The ultimate marriage of spirit and soul, *animus* and *anima*, is the wedding of heaven and earth, our highest ideals and ambitions united with our lowliest symptoms and complaints.[1]

Care of the soul is not a project of self-improvement or a way of being released from the troubles and pains of human existence. It is not at all concerned with living properly or with emotional health. These are the concerns of temporal, heroic, promethean life. Care of the soul touches another dimension, in no way separate from life, but not identical either with the problem solving that occupies so much of our consciousness. We care for the soul solely by honoring its expression, by giving it time and opportunity to reveal itself, and by living life in a way that fosters the depth, interiority, and quality in which it flourishes. Soul is its own purpose and end.

To the soul, memory is more important than planning, art more compelling than reason, and love more fulfilling than understanding. We know we are well on the way toward soul when we feel attachment to the world and the people around us and when we live as much from the heart as from the head. We know soul is being cared for when our pleasures feel deeper than usual, when we can let go of the need to be free of complexity and confusion, and when compassion takes the place of distrust and fear. Soul is interested in the differences among cultures and individuals, and within us it wants to be expressed in uniqueness if not in outright eccentricity.

Therefore, when in the midst of my confusion and my stumbling attempts to live a transparent life, I am the fool, and not everyone around me, and then I know I am discovering the power of the soul to make a life interesting. Ultimately, care of the soul results in an individual 'I' I never would have planned for or maybe even wanted. By caring for the soul faithfully, every day, we step out of the way and let our full genius emerge, soul coalesces into the mysterious philosopher's stone, that rich, solid core of personality the alchemists sought, or it opens into the peacock's tail—a revelation of the soul's colors and a display of its dappled brilliance.[2]

To enter and experience higher dimensions, the soul is enveloped in a radiant garment. The garment is woven out of one's virtuous days. Parallels appear in Islamic and Iranian eschatology—and in Mahayana Buddhism. "Moses ascended in the cloud, was enveloped by the cloud, and was sanctified within the cloud—so as to receive Torah for Israel in holiness." (BT Yoma 42)[3]

The ten fingers of the human hand symbolize the ten *sefirot*. By pouring water generously over the fingers, one stimulates an abundant flow of blessing above.[4] A human being can draw a figure but cannot cast into it breath, soul, bowels, and intestines like G-d. Into the fetus G-d casts a soul, whose different aspects correspond to various *sefirot*. *Hashem* also matches couples which is as difficult for Him as it is for us since the match does not always work out. *Hashem*'s uniting of couples does not just follow Creation, it reenacts Creation. Each human couple constitutes a new world.[5]

When a person raises his hands in prayer or blessing, the right hand (symbolizing *Hesed* or divine right hand) should be higher than the left (symbolizing divine left hand, *Din*), thereby empowering *Hesed* over *Din*.[6]

In the name of Rabbi Simon "You cannot find a single blade of grass that does not have a constellation in the sky, striking it and telling it: 'Grow!'" (Bereshit Rabbah 10:6)[7]

REFERENCES

INTRODUCTION

1. Green, Arthur, Introduction in trans. and commentary *The Zohar Pritzker Edition Volume I* Stanford, CA: Stanford University Press, 2004. p. XXIII
2. Jacobs, Louis *The Jewish Mystics* Jerusalem, Israel: Keter Publishing House, 1976. p. 60
3. ibid. pp. 220-221
4. ibid. pp. 249-250
5. ibid. p. 251
6. Smith, Howard *Let There be light Modern Cosmology and Kabbalah* Novato, CA: New World Library, 2006. p. 138
7. ibid. p. 23
8. ibid. p. 61
9. ibid. p. 69
10. ibid. p. 83
11. ibid. p. 100

12. ibid. pp. 104-105
13. ibid. p. 169
14. Shulman, Jason *Kabbalistic Healing A Path to an Awakened Soul* Rochester, Vermont: Inner Traditions 2004. pp 76-77
15. Smith op. cit. p. 179
16. Shulman op. cit. p. 5
17. ibid. pp 100-101
18. Moore, Thomas *Care of the Soul . . . A Guide for Cultivating Depth* and *Sacredness in Everyday Life* NY: Harper Collins, 1992 p. 170
19. ibid. pp 126-127
20. Matt op. cit. *Volume III* p. 361 1:226a fn 314
21. Green op. cit. *Volume I* p. LXXII
22. ibid. p. 174 1:29b fn 530
23. ibid. p. 385 1:66a fn 331
24. Matt op. cit. *Volume III* p. 531 1:249a fn 987

SEFIROT

1. Green, Arthur, Introduction in trans. and commentary *The Zohar Pritzker Edition Volume I* Stanford, CA: Stanford University Press, 2004. p. LXXIII
2. Smith, Howard *Let There be Light Modern Cosmology* and *Kabbalah* Novato, CA: New World Library 2006. p. 88-89
3. Matt, op. cit. *Volume I* p. XXXVI

4. ibid. p. XLV to LIII
5. Lachower, Fischel and Tishby, Isaiah *The Wisdom of the Zohar . . . An Anthology of Texts Volume I* Portland, Oregon: The Littman Library of Jewish Civilization 2008. p. 192 footnote 365
6. ibid. Volume I p. 250
7. ibid. Volume I p. 273
8. ibid. Volume I p. 288
9. ibid. Volume I p. 371
10. ibid. Volume I p. 426
11. Smith op. cit. p. 97
12. ibid. p. 169
13. Matt op. cit. *Volume V* p. 186 2:126b fn 6
14. ibid. p. 188 2:127a fn 11, 12
15. ibid. p. 191 2:127a fn 18
16. ibid. p. 196 2:127b fn 29, 30
17. ibid. p. 227 2:132a fn 106
18. ibid. p. 141 2:121b fn 4, 5
19. ibid. p. 148 2:122a fn 26, 29
20. Matt op. cit. *Volume II* p. 59 1:87b fn 462
21. Matt op. cit. *Volume VI* p. 21 2:182b fn 53
22. ibid. p. 21 2:182b fn 54
23 ibid. p. 319 2:229b fn 164
24. Matt op. cit. *Volume VII* p. 401 3:61B fn 134
25. ibid. Preface

26. ibid. p. 3 3:4a fn 5
27. ibid. p. 53 3:10b fn 158
28. ibid. p. 53 fn 159
29. ibid. p. 54 fn 160
30. ibid. p. 54 fn 161

PROPHETS

1. Matt, Daniel Chanan, trans. and commentary *The Zohar Pritzker Edition Volume I* Stanford, CA: Stanford University Press, 2004. p. 63 1:9b fn 476
2. Jacobs, Louis *The Jewish Mystics* Jerusalem, Israel: Keter Publishing House, 1976. p. 28
3. Matt op. cit. *Volume IV* p. 358 2:65b fn 560
4. Matt op. cit. *Volume V* p. 376 2:150b fn 529, 530
5. Matt op. cit. *Volume VI* p. 121 2:197a fn 40

DEMONS, DEVILS, SATAN, EVIL

1. Matt, Daniel Chanan, trans. and commentary *The Zohar Pritzker Edition Volume V* Stanford, CA: Stanford University Press, 2009. p. 369 2:149b fn 508
2. ibid. *Volume IV* p. 105 2:27b fn 128
3. Matt op cit. *Volume V* p. 572 2:178b fn 67
4. Matt op. cit. *Volume I* p. 64 1:9b fn 478

5. Matt op. cit. *Volume V* p. 376 2:150b fn 529
6. ibid. p. 7 2:95b fn 20
7. Matt op. cit. *Volume III* p. 211 1:198a fn 193
8. Matt op. cit. *Volume V* p. 507 173a fn 902, 903, 904
9. Matt op. cit. *Volume I* p. 137 1:18a fn 225
10. Matt op. cit. *Volume V* p. 376 2:150b fn 530
11. Matt op. cit. *Volume IV* p. 353 2:65a fn 544
12. Matt op. cit. *Volume V* p. 294 fn 291
13. Matt op. cit. *Volume V* p. 294 2:141a fn 292
14. ibid. p. 295 2:141a fn 294
15. Lachower, Fischel and Tishby, Isaiah *The Wisdom of the Zohar . . . An Anthology of Texts Volume II* Portland, Oregon: The Littman Library of Jewish Civilization. 2008 p. 464
16. Lachower op. cit. Volume III p. 1435
17. Lachower op. cit. Volume II p. 464
18. Matt op. cit. *Volume III* p. 219 1:199a fn 246
19. Matt op. cit. *Volume V* p. 170 2:125a fn 87
20. Matt op. cit. *Volume III* p. 162 1:190b fn 490
21. ibid. p. 239 1:202a fn 361
22. Lachower op. cit. *Volume I* p. 188
23. Matt op. cit *Volume VI* p.16 2:181b fn 43
24. Matt op. cit *Volume I* p. 230 1:36b fn 997, 999
25. Matt op. cit. *Volume V* p. 13 2:96b fn 38
26. ibid. p. 17 2:97a fn 46

27. ibid. p. 114 2:113a fn 321, 322
28. ibid. p. 117 2:106a fn 330
29. ibid. p. 131 2:108b fn 369, 370, 371
30. Matt op. cit. *Volume I* p. 296 1:53b fn 1429
31. Matt, op. cit. *Volume II* p. 146 1:106a fn 232
32. Matt op. cit. *Volume VI.* p. 18 2:182a fn 49
33. ibid. p. 68 2:189b fn 38
34. ibid. p. 343 2:233b fn 241
35. ibid. p. 87 2:192b fn 88
36. ibid. p. 221 2:214b fn 339
37. Matt op. cit. *Volume III* p. 27 1:170a fn 180 and *Volume III* p. 27 1:170a fn 184
38. Matt op. cit. *Volume I* p. 40 1:6b fn 275 and *Volume I* p. 40 1:6b fn 279
39. Matt op. cit. *Volume VII* p. 305 3:48b fn 160
40. Matt op. cit. *Volume VII* p. 183 3:31b fn 50

NUMBERS, COLORS, HEBREW LETTERS and WORDS

1. Matt, Daniel Chanan, trans. and commentary *The Zohar Pritzker Edition Volume VI* Stanford, CA: Stanford University Press, 2011. p. 324 2:230b fn 180
2. ibid. *Volume I* p. 286 1:51b fn 1365

3. Kushner, Lawrence and Polen, Nehemia *Killing Words with Light . . . Hasidic* and *Mystical Reflections on Jewish Prayer* Woodstock, VT: Jewish Lights Publishing, 2004. p. 9
4. Matt op. cit. *Volume VI* p. 54 2:187a fn 143
5. Matt op. cit. *Volume VII* p. 183 3:31b fn 52
6. Matt op. cit. *Volume I* p. 18 1:3b fn 120
7. Matt op. cit. *Volume I* p. 82 1:12a fn 622, 623
8. Matt op. cit. *Volume IV* p. 27 2.8a fn 110
9. Matt op. cit. *Volume V* p. 333 2:146b fn 401
10. Matt op. cit. *Volume V* p. 385 2:152a fn 556
11. Matt op. cit. *Volume IV* p. 344 2:63b fn 514
12. Matt op. cit. *Volume II* p. 180 1:117a fn 496, 498, 500, 502
13. Matt op. cit. *Volume VI* p. 193 2:209b fn 253
14. Matt op. cit. *Volume IV* p. 499 2:88a fn 480
15. Matt op. cit. *Volume V* p. 314 2:144a fn 350
16. Matt op. cit. *Volume VI* p. 320 2:229b fn 167
17. Matt op. cit. *Volume I* p. 40 1:6b fn 274
18. Matt op. cit. *Volume V* p. 524 2:175b fn 952
19. Matt op. cit. *Volume VI* p. 173 2:206a fn 194
20. Matt op. cit. *Volume IV* p. 424 2:78b fn 195
21. Matt op. cit. *Volume III* p. 471 1:241a fn 785
22. Matt op. cit. *Volume IV* p. 39 2:10a fn 172
23. Matt op. cit. *Volume IV* p. 54-55 2:12a fn 238, 241, 243
24. Matt op. cit. *Volume III* p. 469 1:240b fn 779

25. Matt op. cit. *Volume V* p. 550 2:176b fn 11
26. Matt op. cit. *Volume VII* p. 47 3:9b fn 144
27. Matt op. cit. *Volume IV* p. 338 2:62b fn 495
28. Matt op. cit. *Volume IV* p. 469 2:84a fn 369
29. Matt op. cit. *Volume II* p. 7 1:78a fn 41
30. Matt op. cit. *Volume II* p. 32 1:83b fn 237, 238, 239, 240
31. Matt op. cit. *Volume VI* p. 316 2:229b fn 159
32. Matt op. cit. *Volume VI* p. 299 2:226b fn 106
33. Matt op. cit. *Volume VI* p. 316 2:229b fn 158
34. Matt op. cit. *Volume VI* p. 318 2:229b fn 163
35. Matt op. cit. *Volume VI* p. 318 2:229b fn 164
36. Matt op. cit. *Volume VI* p. 343 2:233b fn 242
37. Matt op. cit. *Volume VI* p. 348 2:234a fn 254
38. Matt op. cit. *Volume IV* p. 364 2:66b fn 583
39. Matt op. cit. *Volume IV* p. 85 2:27a fn 52, 53, 54
40. Matt op. cit. *Volume V* p. 390 2:152b fn 571
41. Matt op. cit. *Volume V* p. 572 2:178b fn 65, 66
42. Matt op. cit. *Volume III* p. 82 1:178b fn 545, 547
43. Matt op. cit. *Volume III* p. 439 1:237a fn 657
44. Matt op. cit. *Volume IV* p. 523 2:91a fn 568, 570, 571
45. Matt op. cit. *Volume V* p. 387 2:152a fn 561, 562
46. Matt op. cit. *Volume VII* p. 210 3:36a fn 9
47. Matt op. cit. *Volume VII* p. 219 3:37a fn 43
48. Matt op. cit. *Volume VII* p. 233 3:39a fn 81
49. Matt op. cit. *Volume VII* p. 429 3:65b fn 225

CHARACTERS—FROM CREATION THROUGH 1200 CE

1. Matt, Daniel Chanan, trans. and commentary *The Zohar Pritzker Edition Volume IV* Stanford, CA: Stanford University Press, 2007 p. 153 2:34b fn 54
2. Lachower, Fischel and Tishby, Isaiah *The Wisdom of the Zohar . . . An Anthology of Texts Volume II* Portland, Oregon: The Littman Library of Jewish Civilization. 2008 p. 562
3. ibid. Volume III p. 1081
4. ibid. Volume I p. 197
5. Matt op. cit. *Volume V* p. 412 2:156a fn 640
6. Matt op. cit. *Volume IV* p. 257 2:51b fn 213
7. Lachower op. cit. *Volume II* p. 590
8. ibid. *Volume II* p. 511
9. Matt op. cit. *Volume IV* p. 188 2:39a fn 172
10. Lachower op. cit. *Volume III* p. 1090
11. Matt op. cit. *Volume VI* p. 329 2:229b fn 196
12. Matt op. cit. *Volume I* p. 298 1:53b fn 1438
13. Matt op. cit. *Volume V* p. 473.168a fn 804, 805
14. Matt op. cit. *Volume I* p. 221 1:35b fn 929
15. Matt op. cit. *Volume I* p. 315 1:56a fn 1544
16. Lachower op. cit. *Volume II* p. 631
17. Matt op. cit. *Volume III* p. 136 1:186b fn 324

18. Lachower op. cit. *Volume III* p. 1421
19. Matt op. cit. *Volume II* p.5 1:77b fn 34
20. ibid. *Volume II* p. 209 1:123a fn 48
21. ibid. *Volume II* p. 219 1:127a fn 129
22. ibid. *Volume II* p. 222 1:128a fn 147
23. Matt op. cit. *Volume V* p. 330 2:146a fn 392
24. Matt op. cit. *Volume II* p. 163 1:112a fn 363
25. Matt op. cit. *Volume III* p. 121 1:184a fn 230
26. Matt op. cit. *Volume II* p. 185 1:118b fn 539-541
27. Matt, op. cit. *Volume III* p. 67 1:176b fn 454-455
28. Matt op. cit. *Volume II* p. 209 1:123a fn 49
29. Matt op. cit. *Volume I* p. 163 1:21b fn 447
30. ibid. p. 296 1:53b fn 1429
31. Matt op. cit. *Volume II* p. 189 1:119a fn 572
32. Matt op. cit. *Volume III* p. 32 1:171a fn 220, 223
33. ibid. p. 51 1:174a fn 364, 368, 369
34. Ibid. p. 44 1:173a fn 316, 317, 320
35. ibid. P. 58 1:175a fn 412-413
36. ibid. p. 117 1:183b fn 211
37. ibid. p. 134 1:186a fn 311
38. ibid. p. 486 1:243a fn 838
39. ibid. p. 497 1:244b fn 881-882
40. Matt op. cit. *Volume VII* p. 478 3:71b fn 387
41. Matt op. cit. *Volume III* p. 504 1:246a fn 903
42. Matt op. cit. *Volume IV* p. 60 2:12b fn 264

43. ibid. p. 77 2:23a fn 27
44. ibid. p. 116 2:29b fn 178
45. ibid. p. 128 2:31a fn 215-216
46. Lachower op.cit. *Volume II* p. 483
47. Matt op. cit. *Volume IV* p. 190 2:39b fn 179-181
48. Matt op. cit. *Volume II* p. 364 1:154b fn 359-360
49. Matt op. cit. *Volume VI* p. 278 2:223b fn 48
50. ibid. p. 75 2:190b fn 57
51. Matt op. cit. *Volume V* p. 330 2:146a fn 395
52. Lachower op. cit. *Volume III* p. 1423
53. Matt op. cit. *Volume VI* p. 240 2:217b fn 404
54. Matt op. cit. *Volume IV* p. 79 2:23a fn 33
55. ibid. p. 76 2:23a fn 22
56. ibid. p. 265 2:52b fn 234
57. Lachower op. cit. *Volume I* p. 231
58. ibid. p. 250
59. Matt op. cit. *Volume VII* p. 198 3:34b fn 99
60. ibid. p. 16 3:5b fn 46
61. ibid. p. 16 3:5b fn 47
62. ibid. p. 403 3:61b fn 139
63. ibid. p. 534 3:78b fn 554
64. Matt op. cit. *Volume IV* p. 84 2:24a fn 50
65. Matt op. cit. *Volume III* p. 521 1:248a fn 955
66. Matt op. cit. *Volume II* p. 292 1:142b fn 253
67. Matt op. cit. *Volume V* p. 384 2:166a fn 552

68. Matt op. cit. *Volume II* p. 169 1:113b fn 407

69. Matt op. cit. *Volume IV* p. 242 2:49b fn 165

70. Matt op. cit. *Volume I* p. 70 1:10b fn 526

71. Matt op. cit. *Volume II* p.189 1:119a fn 570

72. Matt op. cit. *Volume IV* p. 36-37 2.9b fn 163-166

73. Matt op. cit. *Volume VI* p. 221 2:214b fn 338

74. Matt op. cit. *Volume V* p. 519 175a 71 fn 937

75. ibid. p. 533 2:176b fn 984

76. Lachower op. cit. *Volume III* p. 1160

77. ibid. p. 1355

78. ibid. p. 1362

79. Matt op. cit. *Volume IV* p. 266 2:52b fn 236

PLACES/THINGS—GARDEN OF EDEN, MACHPELAH, BABEL, CLOUD, FLOOD

1. Matt, Daniel Chanan, trans. and commentary *The Zohar Pritzker Edition Volume IV* Stanford, CA: Stanford University Press, 2011. pp. 150-151 2:34b fn 45-46

2. ibid. *Volume V* pp. 484-487 2:169b fn 835-841

3. ibid. *Volume V* p. 512 2:174a fn 917

4. ibid. *Volume V* p. 1 2:94b fn 3

5. ibid. *Volume V* p. 160 2:123b fn 59-60

6. Matt op. cit. *Volume VI* p. 195 2:209b fn 258

7. Matt op. cit. *Volume VI* p. 200 2:210b fn 274

8. Matt op. cit. *Volume VI* p. 201 2:211a fn 277
9. Matt op. cit. *Volume VI* p. 201 2:211a fn 278
10. Matt op. cit. *Volume VI* p. 206 2:211b fn 291
11. Matt op. cit. *Volume II* p. 215 1:125b fn 96
12. Matt op. cit. *Volume I* p. 69 1:10b fn 525
13. Matt op. cit. *Volume IV* pp. 284-285 2:55a fn 305
14. ibid. *Volume IV* p. 321 2:60b fn 432
15. Matt op. cit. *Volume VI* p. 99 2:194a fn 118
16. Matt op. cit. *Volume V* p. 418 2:157a fn 651
17. Lachower, Fischel and Tishby, Isaiah *The Wisdom of the Zohar . . . An Anthology of Texts Volume I* Portland, Oregon: The Littman Library of Jewish Civilization, 2008. p. 188 fn 334
18. ibid. *Volume I* p. 188 fn 335
19. ibid. *Volume I* p. 188 fn 338
20. Matt op. cit. *Volume V* p. 300 2:141b fn 305
21. Matt op. cit. *Volume V* pp. 338-339 2:62b-263a fn 496-497
22. Matt op. cit. *Volume V* p. 394 2:153a fn 586
23. Lachower op. cit. *Volume I* p. 188 fn 339
24. Matt op. cit. *Volume V* p. 156 2:123a fn 46
25. Matt op. cit. *Volume VI* p.5 2:180a fn 15
26. Matt op. cit. *Volume III* p. 544 1:25a fn 1029
27. Matt op. cit. *Volume V* p. 422 2:157b fn 660
28. Matt op. cit. *Volume VII* p. 233 3:39a fn 82

29. Matt op. cit. *Volume IV* p. 273 2:53b fn 260
30. Matt op. cit. *Volume VII* pp. 65-69 3:12a-3:12b fn 201-212
31. Matt op. cit. *Volume V* p. 133 2:113b fn 375
32. Matt op. cit. *Volume V* p. 3 2:95a fn 8
33. Matt op. cit. *Volume V* p. 422 157b fn 658
34. Matt op. cit. *Volume VI* p. 405 2:242b fn 419
35. Jacobs, Louis *The Jewish Mystics* Jerusalem, Israel: Keter Publishing House, 1976. pp. 50-52
36. Matt op. cit. *Volume VII* p. 74 3:13a fn 228
37. Matt op. cit. *Volume VII* p. 314 3:49b fn 189
38. Matt op. cit. *Volume VII* p. 380 3:59a fn 75
39. Matt op. cit. *Volume VII* pp. 539-540 3:79a fn 567

ANGELS

1. Matt, Daniel Chanan, trans. and commentary *The Zohar Pritzker Edition Volume I* Stanford, CA: Stanford University Press, 2004. p. 325 1:57b fn 1597
2. ibid. p. 67 1:10a fn 502
3. Matt op. cit. *Volume VI* p. 152 2:202b fn 127
4. Matt op. cit. *Volume I* p. 237 1:37b fn 1041
5. Matt op. cit. *Volume II* p. 138 1:104a fn 169, 173
6. Matt op. cit. *Volume II* p. 324 1:148a fn 33

7. Matt op. cit. *Volume III* p. 260 1:205b fn 16
8. Matt op. cit. *Volume V* p. 350 2:277b fn 453
9. Matt op. cit. *Volume V* p. 582 2:179a fn 88
10. Lachower, Fischel and Tishby, Isaiah *The Wisdom of the Zohar . . . An Anthology of Texts* Portland, Oregon: The Littman Library of Jewish Civilization. 2008 *Volume II* p. 631
11. Matt op. cit. *Volume III* p. 398 1:231b fn 479-480
12. Matt op. cit. *Volume III* p. 399-400 1:231b fn 485-488
13. Matt op. cit. *Volume IV* p.88 2:24b fn 64
14. Matt op. cit. *Volume IV* pp. 420-421 2:78b fn 185-188
15. Matt op. cit. *Volume IV* p. 38 2:9b fn 167, 170
16. Matt op. cit. *Volume V* p. 136 2:114a fn 381
17. Matt op. cit. *Volume V* p. 239 2:133b fn 140
18. Matt op. cit. *Volume V* p. 572 2:178b fn 67
19. Lachower op. cit. *Volume II* p. 631
20. Matt op. cit. *Volume VII* p. 335 3:53a fn 12
21. Matt op. cit. *Volume VII* p. 454 3:68b fn 300
22. Lachower op. cit. *Volume II* p. 648
23. Lachower op. cit. *Volume II* p. 684
24. Lachower op. cit. *Volume III* p. 883
25. Lachower op. cit. *Volume III* p. 887
26. Lachower op. cit. *Volume II* p. 812
27. Jacobs, Louis *The Jewish Mystics* Jerusalem, Israel: Keter Publishing House, 1976. pp. 251-252

CIRCUMCISION, SOULS, REINCARNATION AND RESURRECTION

1. Matt, Daniel Chanan, trans. and commentary *The Zohar Pritzker Edition Volume I* Stanford, CA: Stanford University Press, 2004. p. 91 1:13a fn 688
2. ibid. p. 139 1:18b fn 245
3. Matt op. cit. *Volume II* p. 86 1:93a fn 657, 658, 662
4. Matt op. cit. *Volume III* p. 508 1:246b fn 915
5. Lachower, Fischel and Tishby, Isaiah *The Wisdom of the Zohar . . . An Anthology of Texts Volume I* Portland, Oregon: The Littman Library of Jewish Civilization. 2008 p. 190
6. Matt op. cit. *Volume VI* p. 18 2:182a fn 49
7. Matt op. cit. Matt, *Volume I* p. 117 1:16a fn 67
8. Matt op. cit. *Volume IV* p. 503 2:89a fn 496
9. Matt op. cit. Vo*lume III* p. 142 1:187b fn 365
10. Matt op. cit. *Volume IV* p. 507 2:89b fn 513
11. Matt op. cit. *Volume IV* p. 479 2:85b fn 407
12. Matt op. cit. *Volume IV* p. 23 2:7a fn 88
13. Matt op. cit. *Volume I* p. 80 1:12a fn 608
14. Matt op. cit. *Volume III* p. 410 1:233a fn 538
15. Matt op. cit. *Volume III* p. 103 1:181b fn 120-121

16. Matt op. cit. *Volume III* p. 144 1:187b fn 376
17. Matt op. cit. *Volume IV* p. 83 2:23b fn 46, 49
18. Spitz, Rabbi Elie Kaplan *Does the Soul Survive? A Jewish Journey to Belief in Afterlife, Past Lives* and *Living with Purpose* Woodstock, Vermont: Jewish Lights Publishing. 2011 p. 43
19. ibid. p. 44
20. ibid. pp. 45-46
21. ibid. pp. 46-47
22. ibid. pp. 52-53
23. ibid. pp. 85-86
24. ibid. pp. 211-212
25. ibid. p. 140
26. ibid. pp. 160-161
27. ibid. p. 164
28. Matt op. cit. *Volume VI* p. 197 2:210a fn 266
29. Matt op. cit. *Volume VI* p. 35 2:184b fn 87
30. Matt op. cit. *Volume VI* p. 256 2:220a fn 454
31. Matt op. cit. *Volume VII* p. 41 3:9a fn 126
32. Matt op. cit. *Volume VII* p. 266 3:43b fn 31
33. Matt op. cit. *Volume VII* p. 334 3:53a fn 11
34. Matt op. cit. *Volume VII* p. 469 3:70b fn 354 fn 355
35. Matt op. cit. *Volume VII* p. 479 3:71b fn 389

CONCLUDING THOUGHTS

1. Moore, Thomas *Care of the Soul . . . A Guide for Cultivating Depth* and *Sacredness in Everyday Life* New York, NY: Harper Collins 1992 pp. 262-263
2. ibid. pp. 304-305
3. Matt, Daniel Chanan, trans. and commentary *The Zohar Pritzker Edition Volume I* Stanford, CA: Stanford University Press, 2012. p. 385 1:66a fn 331, 333
4. ibid. *Volume II* p. 61 1:88a fn 481
5. Matt op. cit. *Volume II* p. 70 1:90b fn 541-545
6. Matt op. cit. *Volume IV* p. 369 2:67a fn 2
7. ibid. *Volume IV* p. 436 2:80b fn 249

GLOSSARY OF HEBREW AND OTHER WORDS

Abba and *Imma*—father and mother

Adam HaRishon—first man. After eating the forbidden fruit *Adam HaRishon* falls into the physical world (*Olam haAssiya*) . . . a lower spiritual plane. Sparks scatter in all directions because *Olam haAssiyah* is filled with profane shards (*kelipot*) from the breaking of the vessels. Some of the sparks are thrust deeper within *Adam haRishon* which he passes on to his descendents. Other sparks fall among the *kelipot*, a scattering that leaves *Adam haRishon* and G-d, the source of the sparks, incomplete.

Adam Kadmon—primordial man. The *sefirot* take the form of pillars which constitute *Adam Kadmon* the primordial human which is the root of the vessels themselves. *Adam Kadmon* is in the realm above the highest spiritual levels of the world known as *Atzilut*. All on the level of divine self-creation is perfect.

Adamah—ground

Adonai—G-d

Aggadah or *Haggadah*—comes from the Aramaic for tales, lore and refers to the homiletic and non-legalistic exegetical texts in the classical rabbinic literature of Judaism, particularly as recorded in the Talmud and Midrash. In general, *Aggadah* is a compendium of rabbinic homilies that incorporates folklore, historical anecdotes, moral exhortations, and practical advice in various spheres, from business to medicine.

ahavah—love

alef—first letter of the 22 letter Hebrew alphabet with a numerical value of one.

Amalekim—A Cannaanite tribe that followed Amalek

Amidah—the standing prayer is the central prayer of the Jewish liturgy usually done silently.

Anakim—a race of giants descended from Anak. They dwelt in the south of Palestine, in the neighbourhood of Hebron (Gen. 23:2).

ani—Hebrew first person singular nominative (I) pronoun.

anima and *animus*—the inner feminine side of a man and the inner masculine side of a woman

aqev—the heel of the foot

arikh anpin—long face/extended countenance also implying "The Infinitely Patient One"

aron—coffin: pious humans are buried in an *aron*

asher—that

asher ehyeh—that I am . . . *asher*, that, is associated with *osher*, happiness, namely the blissful bond between *Hokhmah* and *Binah*

asiyah—the ten spheres of the firmament

Atzilut—the highest spiritual levels of the world

ayin—fifteenth letter of the 22 letter Hebrew alphabet with a numerical value of seventy: Nothingness

b'limah—without anything

b'reit esh—in a covenant of fire

bara—created

bat sheva or *Batsheva*—The story of *Batsheva* and King David appears in the second Book of Samuel. Her name is translated as meaning 'Daughter of The Oath.'

bayit sheni—second Temple or literally second house

benei Yisra'el—path for Jews

be-qittura de-idduna qastira ila'ah—to delightfully bind in the palace of delight

berakhot—benediction

be-rehsit or *bereshit* or *B'Resheit*—in the beginning (i.e., of time itself in a covenant of fire) Hebrew for Genesis. The word *Be-reshit* contains two words: *bara* (created) referring to the hidden mystery of creation, and *shit* (six) referring to the revelation of the six *sefirot*.

berit, berith, bris, briss, brith—the rite of circumcision performed on a male child on the eighth day of his life.

Beriyah, Yezirah, Asiyah—represents three of the four worlds of creation. *Beriyah* or *Briah* as in "creating", *Yezirah* (also known as *Olam Yetsirah*) as in "making," and *Asiyah* or *Atziluth* as in the world of formation.

bet—the second letter of the 22 letter Hebrew alphabet with a numerical value of two; exemplifies interiority

Binah known as *Mi*—who or whom. *Binah* is a *sefira* under *Keter* meaning 'understanding.'

bohu—form: *tohu* and *bohu* refer respectively to primordial matter and form. *Tohu* was seen as the root of evil and *bohu* was the origin of good.

castrum (pl. castra)—Latin for palace

chayah or *yechidah*—the highest levels of the soul which are direct extensions of G-d are unfettered by the soul's lower levels and are able to experience the joy of G-d's presence.

Chuppah—the four sided canopy covering in which wedding ceremonies are conducted

dal—poor

Dalet—fourth letter of the 22 letter Hebrew alphabet with a numerical value of four.

derekh emet—off the true path

deyoqna—the image of this world

Din, Gevurah—judgement

dumah—silence: In *dumah* (literally meaning silence and the name for the netherworld) the corpse is punished by *hibbut ha-quever* (beating in the grave) by the Angel of Death or other heavenly or demonic beings. Most souls are punished in Hell and eventually purified of their sins. After ascending from Hell the soul is bathed and perfumed, and finally offered as a sacrifice by the heavenly angel and priest Michael.

Eden—*Gan Edhen* is the garden of G-d as described in the book of Genesis 2-3.

ehyeh—I am (or I will be)

Ein Sof—infinity: the term *Ein Sof* appears as the hidden source from which the ten *sefirot* emerge. *Ein Sof* originally meant 'endlessly' and is used in a nominal sense to designate 'the Endless' or 'that which is beyond all limits.' "*Ein Sof* refers to the endless and undefinable reservoir of divinity, the ultimate source out of which everything flows. *Ein Sof* is utterly transcendent in the sense that no words can describe it, no mind comprehend it. But it is also ever-present in the sense of the old rabbinic adage 'He is the place of the world.'

El Shaddai—Is one of the Hebrew names for G-d conventionally translated as "G-d Almighty" while the translation of *El* is conventionally known as G-d.

Elohim—*Hashem* (G-d) created the world by Judgment as indicated by the appearance of the name *Elohim* (associated with judgment)

Elohim zulatekha—Oh G-d, but you

emet—truth

erev rav—mixed multitude and refers to "sons of Lilith" *erev rav* souls are a mixture of good and evil.

Five types of *erev rav*:

1. *Amalekim*—followers of Amalek . . . those that survived in the fourth exile were oppressive leaders that opposed Israel with weapons of violence. Balaam and Balak were from the side of Amalek.
2. *Nefilim*—are from the world above and are cast down in order to lust for beautiful women.
3. *Gibborim*—they build and do not for *Hashem* but to make a name for themselves. They build cities, synagogues, schools, etc. and get strength from *sitra otra* (the other side).
4. *Rephaim*—they forsake Israel in bitter straits for they have the power to save but not the desire. They forsake the Torah and those who study it, in order to deal kindly with idolaters.
5. *Anakim*—they despise those of whom it is said 'They shall be necklaces (*anakim*) about your neck.'

erez—earth

ezem ha-shamayim—the essence of heaven

esh—fire

frankincense—whitish resin

Gan Eden—Garden of Eden: In *Gan Eden* the highest levels of the soul (*chayah* or *yechidah*) are direct extensions of G-d and are unfettered by the soul's lower levels and are able to experience the joy of G-d's presence. The lower levels of the soul return to their source (*tzror hachayim*) the storehouse of life where it receives its message for the next reincarnation (*gilgulei neshamot*) that translates to 'the rolling of the souls' from body to body

Gedullah—an alternate name for the *sephirah Chesed*, loving-kindness

Gehenna, Gehinnom or *Gen-hinnom*—Hell: A soul that needs purification by fire is brought to a special place in Hell called *Gen-hinnom* which is also a valley south of Jerusalem where child sacrifices were allegedly offered to Molech and also served to incinerate refuse, dump animal carcasses, and the bodies of criminals. *Ben-Hinnom* serves as a purgatory, so that souls can be cleansed in fire and afterward enter the Garden of Eden.

qets yamin—end of the right

Gevurah—Judgement

gibborim—is glossed as "mightiest" which is an intensive for *gabar* that can be glossed "mighty." Many times it is used of people who are valiant, mighty, or of great stature. There is some confusion between *Gibborim* as a class of beings because of its use in Genesis 6:4.

However, this passage describes the *Nephilim* as mighty (*gibborim*).

gilgulei neshamot—the rolling of the souls from body to body . . . meaning reincarnation

gimel—third letter of the 22 letter Hebrew alphabet with a numerical value of three

gimatriyya or *gematria* is the science of assigning numerical values to Hebrew letters in order to reveal deep associations and meanings, seeking to make clear actual, often hidden, correspondences among ideas, insights, and even physical objects that on the surface have little obvious connection.

ha—the

ha-adam—human being

haggadah—telling, expounding

haleluyah or *hallelujah*—comprises two elements: the divine name *Yah* and directive *halelu* (praise) and is the totality of the holy supernal Name. *Hallel* (praise) alludes to *Shekhinah* who constantly offers praise to the blessed Holy One and is symbolized by the final letter *he* of YHVH and the remaining letters of *haleluyah* consist of the rest of YHVH (*yod, he, vav*)

hallel—praise

hamor—donkey or he-ass

Hanokh—Enoch

ha-olam ha-ba—is the world that is coming. The term is often been understood as referring to the hereafter and often been translated as 'the world to come.' The world that is coming already exists, occupying another dimension. The wise call it *ha-olam ha-ba* not because it does not exist now, but for us today in this world it is still to come. 'The world to come' does not succeed this world in time, but exists from eternity as a reality outside and above time, to which the soul ascends. In kabbalah the 'world that is coming' often refers to *Binah*, the continuous souirce of emanation.

Hashem—G-d

hashmal—(electrum) is portrayed as sparks of flashing and dancing light that cannot be assigned a single fixed form

hasidut—love, devotion . . . *hasidut* leads to Holy Spirit

hata'ah—sin; according to the venerable source Rav Hamnuna Sava *het* and *tet* imply *hata'ah* or sin, which explains why these two letters do not appear in any of the names of the twelve tribes.

Hay or *He*—fifth letter of the 22 letter Hebrew alphabet with a numerical value of five

hayyot—creatures

heikhalot—Seven halls (*hekhalot*) of *livnat ha-sapir* (sapphire pavement)

Hesed—compassion

heled—world

het—eighth letter of the 22 letter Hebrew alphabet with a numerical value of eight

hibbut ha-quever—beating in the grave. In *dumah* (literally meaning silence and the name for the netherworld) the corpse is punished by *hibbut ha-quever* (beating in the grave) by the Angel of Death or other heavenly or demonic beings. Most souls are punished in Hell and eventually purified of their sins. After ascending from Hell the soul is bathed and perfumed, and finally offered as a sacrifice by the heavenly angel and priest Michael.

Hod—majesty or splendor

Hokhamah—wisdom

h-olam ha-ba—the world to come

iddun—delight

idduna—is based on *iddun*, literally delight, and alludes to *Hokhmah*, who is symbolized by *Eden*. When all members dwell in a single bond (*idduna*), delight, of desire—from the head above to below, and out of their delight and desire they all pour into Him, He becomes a river issuing from Eden.

irah—watchful

ishtaniat—changes

izzim—goat hair, goats; *izzim* suggests *sa'ir*, goat, demon, satyr, and the scapegoat sent to the demon Azazel (Leviticus 16).

Goat-hair curtains symbolize powers outside the divine realm that protect the inner, holy powers.

kabbala, kabbalah, qabbala— is an esoteric method, discipline, and school of thought to explain the relationship between an unchanging, eternal and mysterious *Ein Sof* (no end) and the mortal and finite universe that He created.

kaf—eleventh letter of the 22 letter Hebrew alphabet with a numerical value of twenty

kaf final—eleventh letter of the 22 letter Hebrew alphabet with a numerical value of five-hundred

kapporet—gold cover: The divine voice was thought to issue from the space above the *kapporet* and between the two cherubim.

kavannah—intention

kelipot—shards created by G-d when He created the universe: After eating the forbidden fruit *Adam HaRishon* falls into the physical world (*olam haAssiya*) . . . a lower spiritual plane. Sparks scatter in all directions because *olam haAssiyah* is filled with profane shards (*kelipot*) from the breaking of the vessels. Some of the sparks are thrust deeper within *Adam haRishon* which he passes on to this descendents. Other sparks fall among the *kelipot*, a scattering that leaves *Adam haRishon* and G-d, the source of the sparks, incomplete.

Keneset Yisra'el—the legislative branch of the Israeli government

Keter—crown: the highest of the *Sefirot*

Ketubbot—marriage contract

Ketuvim—*w*ritings or Hagiographa . . . the third and final section of the *Tanakh* (Hebrew Bible) after *Torah* (instruction) and *Nevi'im* (prophets)

Klh—company . . . Hebrew root to destroy

kodesh has, kodashim—holy of holies

lamed—the twelfth letter of the Hebrew alphabet with a numerical value of 30. The letter *lamed* in the word *lo* (you shall have) stands taller than all other letters of the alphabet, indicating that G-d alone should be exalted and honored. The image of the upright *lamed* indicates one should not bow down to any false god (Leviticus 19:4). The *alef* or the concluding letter in *lo* has a numerical value of one, indicating G-d's oneness and unity, which must not be compromised or betrayed.

le-ma'an i—for my own sake

lev—heart

levavekha—(double *vet*) your heart

li terumah—offering for or to me

livnat ha-sapir—sapphire pavement

lob—you shall have

lulas and *etrog*—*lulas* are ripe, green, closed frond from a date palm tree. *Etrog* is the fruit of the citron tree. Traditionally at Purim there are three sprigs of myrtle and two willow twigs along with the *lulas* and *etrog* totaling four species, not seven.

luz—light

lvh—Hebrew root to accompany or join

vis—Latin for life force

Malkhut—kingdom

mayim—water

mazzala—constellation of the zodiac or planets

me-ayin—from where

mem—twelfth letter of the 22 letter Hebrew alphabet with a numerical value of forty

mem final—twelfth letter of the 22 letter Hebrew alphabet with a numerical value of six-hundred

merkavah—chariot, divine palaces

Metatron—Enoch's body was to be revealed in heaven in the form of Metatron

mevorakh—blessed, which spell the *rakh*, soft

mi—who or whom

Michael, Gabriel, Raphael—The three archangels are associated respectively with water, fire, and air.

mi-qets yamim—in the course of time

mishkan—Dwelling, Tabernacle

Mishkan ha-Edut—Tabernacle of testimony

mishpat—balanced judgment

mishpatim—laws

mitsvot or *mitzvoth*—commandment or commandments

mor—myrrh

Moriyyah—the mountain in Jerusalem where Issaac was to be sacrificed by his father Abraham

murex trunculus—a violet or bluish purple dye extracted from the gland of the *Murex Trunculus* snail for the *tekhelet* (the colored thread on the tassel of the garment) which resembles the sea, and the sea resembles the sky, and sky resembles the Throne of Glory.

myrrh—is a reddish resin and *frankincense* is whitish

na'ar—youth, lad, servant, deputy

nefesh—soul, animating the human being

nefesh, ruah, and *nehamah*—*nefesh* (soul, animating the human being), *ruah* (spirit, breath), and *neshamah* (breath, soul). Each of the three aspects derives from its own *sefirotic* source: *neshamah* (the holiest aspect of soul)

Nefilim—sons of G-d: Uzza and Azael were cast down into the world as *Nefilim*

nehsiyyah—forgetfulness

neshamah—soul

Netsah—victory or endurance

nogah—brightness

notarikons—is a method of deriving a word, akin to the creation of an acronym *nun*—thirteenth letter of the 22 letter Hebrew alphabet with a numerical value of sixty

nun final—thirteenth letter of the 22 letter Hebrew alphabet with a numerical value of seven-hundred

ofannim—wheels as seen in Ezekiel's vision

olah—that which ascends The *olah* (ascent offering) ascending to the *sefirot* above *Shekhinah* must be male. The offerings must be *tamim* meaning blameless, complete, intact, free of blemish, impeccable, perfect.

olam baba—in the Messianic Era or the world to come the body will not necessarily need food or water. We will bask in G-d's light like Moshe did for forty days and nights. Our united body and soul is a microcosm of the universe and an essential part of G-d's plan.

olam haAssiya or *olam haAssiyah*—the physical world . . . a lower physical plane

olam hatikkum—reconstituted world: To re-create the divine realm of *yetzirah*, *Adam kadmon* mates internally, thereby allowing for a reconstituted world. *Adam Kadmon* still consists of ten *sefirot* now organized into five faces (*partzufim*) composed of five main *sefirot*: *Keter*; *Chochmah*; *Binah* (that face each other). *Tiferet* and *Malkhut* (which below were back-to-back but are raised by *Keter* to return face-to-face). Adam of the Torah is *Adam HaRishon* formed through the merger of *Binah* and *Tiferet* as they rise up to *Keter* and *Chokhman*. *Adam HaRishon* was supposed to return to *Malkhut* and *Tiferet* face-to-face on the lower level, so as to make an uninterrupted chain of *tikkum* from *Ein Sof* to the lower levels.

onah—conjugal rights

osher—happiness, namely the blissful bond between *Hokhmah* and *Binah*

Pardes—A mnemonic from the words *peshat, re'ayah, derash,* and *sod*. The *Shekhinah* is called the *Pardes* of the Torah . . . She comprises the *peshat* (plain, simple or the direct meaning), *re'ayah* or *remez* (hints or the deep allegoric: hidden or symbolic meaning beyond just the literal sense), *derash* (to inquire, seek), *sod* (secret, mystery, or the esoteric/mystical meaning, as given through inspiration or revelation) which makes the mnemonic *Pardes*.

partzufim—five faces of *Adam Kadmon* consisting of ten *sefirot* organized into five faces (*partzufim*) composed of five main *sefirot*: *Keter; Chochmah; Binah* (that face each other). *Tiferet* and *Malkhut* (which below were back-to-back but are raised by *Keter* to return face-to-face).

Pe—seventeenth letter of the 22 letter Hebrew alphabet with a numerical value of seventy

Pe final—seventeenth letter of the 22 letter Hebrew alphabet with a numerical value of eight-hundred

peri'ah—The act of tearing and pulling back the membrane of the penis in circumcision. In the ritual of circumcision, the foreskin is cut and removed first, disclosing the mucous membrane, which is torn down the center and pulled back, revealing the corona. The act of tearing and pulling back the membrane is called *peri'ah* or uncovering the corona.

peshat, re'ayah, derash, and *sod*—*peshat* (plain, simple or the direct meaning), *re'ayah* or *remez* (hints or the deep allegoric: hidden or symbolic meaning beyond just the literal sense), *derash* (to inquire, seek), *sod* (secret, mystery, or the esoteric/mystical meaning, as given through inspiration or revelation)

qastira—derives from Latin *castrum* (pl. *castra*), castle, fortress, military camp, and symbolizes *Binah*, who is often pictured as a palace or house.

qedushah, kedushah—holy . . . traditionally the third section of the *Amidah* prayer

qelalah—curse

qelippah—husk

qodesh—apartness, sacredness

qodesh la'YHVH—sacredness of G-d

qof—nineteenth of the 22 letter Hebrew alphabet with a numerical value of one hundred. *Qof* is a letter that alludes to the demonic realm, perhaps because it begins the *qelippah* (husk), *qelalah* (curse), *qof* (ape), or conceivably because its numerical value (100) is equivalent to *samekh*, *mem*, an abbreviation of *Samma'el* (Samael), another name for Satan.

qtr—to tie, bind

rahamin—compassion

rakh—edition

ratson, razon—will, favor, good will

reiqanin—the empty ones,

Rephaim—unusually tall/large individuals as described in the Torah

resh—the twentieth letter of the 22 letter Hebrew alphabet with a numerical value of two-hundred: *resh* exemplifies movement, the head, or the beginning of a new enterprise.

resheit—the beginning

ruach or *ruah*—spirit, breath

rum—height, loftiness

sa'ir—goat, demon, satyr, and the scapegoat sent to the demon Azazel (Leviticus 16)

samekh mem—from the abbreviation for the angel of death

Samma'el or *Samael*—is the serpent rider who copulated with Eve and she conceived Cain. Cain is referred to as the 'son of slime' since he was born from the union of the serpent and Eve. Afterward Adam copulated with her and she conceived Abel. Even Abel was not fully refined, since he was still tainted by the demonic. Seth, the third child of Adam and Eve, generated the righteous.

Sefer Raziel—the Book of Raziel: Raziel transmitted a magical book to Adam. Later, probably in the seventeenth century, *Sefer Raziel* (the Book of Raziel) was compiled in its present form, comprising ancient magical, mystical, and cosmological teachings.

Sefer Torah—Book of the Torah

Sefer Yetsirah—the Book of Formation

sefira or *sefirah* or *sefiro*—pertaining to one of the Ten *Sefirot*

sefirotic—pertaining to the *Sefirot*

Sefirot—The ten emanations of G-d in the physical world. The Ten *Sefirot* are described as being 'without concreteness' (*b'limah*, literally, 'without anything') The Ten Sefirot are as follows:

Center *Keter*—Crown, Will, *Ayin* (Nothingness)

Left *Binah*—Understanding, Palace, Womb

Right *Hokhmah*—Wisdom, Primordial Point, Beginning

Left *Gevurah*—Power, *Din* (Judgment), Rigor, Red, Fire, Left Arm, Isaac

Right *Hesed*—Love, *Gedullah* (Greatness), Grace, White, Water, Right Arm, Abraham

Center *Tif'eret*—Beauty, *Rahamim* (Compassion), Blessed Holy One, Heaven, Sun, Harmony, King, Green, Torso, Jacob, Moses

Left *Hod*—Splendor, Prophecy, Left Leg

Right *Netsah*—Endurance, Prophecy, Right Leg

Center *Yesod*—Foundation, *Tsaddiq* (Righteous One), Covenant, Phallus, Joseph

Center *Malkhut*—Kingdom *Shekhinah* (Presence), Assembly of Israel, Earth, Moon, queen, apple orchard, King David, Rachel

Semech, Samekh—fourteenth letter of the 22 letter Hebrew alphabet with a numerical value of sixty

sfr—a root meaning to count, number, to recount, tell, narrate

Sha'arei Gan Eden—Gates of the Garden of Eden

Shabbat—Sabbath

Shamayim—heaven, *ezem ha-shamayim* (the essence of heaven)

shaniat—varies

she'ol—pit

Shekhinah—light . . . *Shekhinah* emerged from the womb of *Binah*, She is called 'the Tree of Knowledge of Good and Evil,' since both Mercy and Power are active in her. The verse in Exodus about gazing at a rainbow actually refers to a vision of the rainbow whose colors convey the hidden *sefirotic* spectrum of *Shekhinah*.

shema—hear

shemittah—release . . . every seventh year is a Sabbatical (*shemittah* or release) during which the land must lie fallow (*yovel*) Just as the seventh year (*shemittah*) releases one year in seven by letting the earth lie fallow. In the cosmic Jubilee all will be drawn back to the Divine Mother to their original place . . . just as in the biblical Jubilee year (every 50 years) all property returns to its original owner.

shemittot—mysticism

shenei asa or *sheneim asar*—twelve indicating the full holiness of *Shekhinah*

Sheqel ha-Qodesh—Moses De Leon wrote the *Sefer Sheqel ha-Qodesh* (Sources and Studies in the Literature of Jewish Mysticism)

shesh—linen or six: According to Exodus 39:27, the tunic worn by all the priests was made of *shesh*, linen. The word *shesh* can also mean six and according to rabbinic tradition, the linen yarn used in the Dwelling consisted of six strands. Six can allude to the six *sefirot* from *Hesed* through *Yesod*, the first of which is symbolized by the priest. By wearing these garments of *shesh*, the priest is arrayed, as it were, in all *shesh sefirot*.

Shet—Seth

Shevirat HaKelim—the shattering of the vessels: The divine light was too powerful and the vessels exploded as a product of G-d's plan. Holy sparks flew in all directions and were dispersed among the broken shards. This is the "Big Bang" theory in physics.

shin—twenty-first letter of the 22 letter Hebrew alphabet with a numerical value of three-hundred.

Shir Ta'eb—a song of desire by rearranging the letters of "in a covenant of fire" *B'reit Esh*

shit—six

shoshanah—lily

sitra ahra—The force of evil is *sitra ahra*, 'the other side'

tamim—blameless, complete, intact, free of blemish, impeccable, perfect . . . as in sacrificing.

tav—twenty-second and last letter of the 22 letter Hebrew alphabet with a numerical value of four-hundred

tefillah shel rosh—the knot of the *tefillah shel rosh* (phylactery worn on the head) is in the shape of the letter *dalet*

tekhelet—refers to a violet or bluish purple dye extracted from the gland of the *Murex Trunculus* snail. Whoever fulfills the commandment of wearing the *tzitzit* (Numbers 15:38-40) is as though he greeted the face of *Shekhinah* for the *tekhelet* (the colored thread on the tassel of the garment) resembles the sea, and the sea resembles the sky, and sky resembles the Throne of Glory.

teli—dragon

Tenakh—full Hebrew bible consisting of *Torah* (Five books of Moshe), *Nevi'im* or Prophets, and *Ketuvim* or writings

terumah—offering

teshuvah—repentance

tet—ninth letter of the 22 letter Hebrew alphabet with a numerical value of nine

Tiferet ha-adam—the (divine) human, Primordial Adam . . . is a tree planted in the field of *Shekhinah*, who is Herself known as 'field of holy apples.' When besieging a town one is not to destroy its fruit

Tiferet—beauty or glory

Tiferet Yisra'el—Beauty of Israel

tikkum—repair: G-d reconstituted enough of the broken shards to enable people to help G-d continue the repair. Human beings would be given the capacity, free will, and duty to help gather the holy sparks. Such extraction of sparks from the shards would be achieved by the doing of G-d's decrees (*mitzvoth*) with proper intention (*kavannah*). By eating the forbidden fruit Adam fell several spiritual levels and some of the sparks were displaced more deeply into Adam's body. All humans begin life with soul sparks originating with Adam.

tikkum from *ein sof*—healing from no end

Tit ha-Yaven—Miry Clay

Tohu—matter: *Tohu* and *Bohu* refer respectively to primordial matter and form. *Tohu* was seen as the root of evil and *bohu* was the origin of good.

Torah—The five books of Moshe given directly by G-d. The four ways of interpreting the Torah are the four rivers that branched out of the river that flowed from Eden. The

Torah (outline of *Sefirot*) has a head, body, heart, mouth, and organs just as Israel has. Israel is the wick, the Torah is the oil, and the *Shekhinah* is the flame.

tov—good

tsaddiq—conveyer of divine

tsadi—eigteenth letter of the 22 letter Hebrew alphabet with a numerical value of ninety

tsadi final—eigteenth letter of the 22 letter Hebrew alphabet with a numerical value of nine-hundred

tselem—image, an ethereal body. Before entering a human body, each soul exists in the Garden of Eden, where s/he is clothed in this *tselem*, which resembles the physical body s/he will inhabit on earth.

tsits—medallion (or plate, rosette), was a gold plate worn on the forehead of the high priest over his turban, bearing the inscription *qodesh la'YHVH*, Holy to *YHVH*. Rabbi Shim'on relates the word *tsits* to the verbal root *tsuts*, to look, peek, peer, gaze. He proceeds to explain how the *tsits* enabled the high priest to determine a person's character.

tsitsit or *tzitzit*—(Numbers 15:38-40) literally fringes . . . to wear fringes on one's garments.

tzimtzum—contraction: G-d withdrew inwardly to create a sphere of emptiness into which G-d could craft creation. G-d finished vessels in the void into which G-d emanated a divine ray of light.

tzror hachayim—storehouse of life . . . the lower levels of the soul return to their source (*tzror hachayim*) the storehouse of life

Urim and *Tummim*—means lights and perfections or, by taking the phrase allegorically, as meaning revelation and truth, or doctrine and truth. The breastplate and the ephod, as well as the *Urim* and *Tummim*, represent *Tiferet* and *Malkhut*, and the rings that join the breastplate and the ephod together are formed through the mystery of the *Ofannim* and the *Hayyot*, which assist *Shekhinah* to achieve intercourse. Therefore when the priest puts these clothes on he is like the supernal image. The stones in the breastplate and the ephod testify to the High Priest's righteousness or his wickedness, while with the gold plate on his forehead the High Priest is able to tell whether the person he is facing is righteous or wicked. Even the most hardened sinners are moved to contrition when they look upon this gold plate, and if they go on to repent their sins are forgiven.

va-ani—and or as for me

vav—sixth letter of the 22 letter Hebrew alphabet with a numerical value of six

vis—Latin for life force

Yah—name for G-d

Yehudah—Judah

Yesod—is also designated as *berit* or covenant, She is also *Keneset Yisra'el*, the embodied 'Community (or: Assembly) of Israel' itself, identified with the Jewish people

yetzirah—Splendor

Yetzirat Ha-Vlad—A medieval text *Seder Yetzirat Ha-Vlad* (the Creation of the Embryo) gives the image of a life preview as a preparation for rebirth

YHV—first three letters of G-d's name

YHVH *Elohim*—name for G-d

yirah—fear

y-irah-v—Taste and see that G-d is good . . . Nothing is lacking to those who are in awe

yitman'un—will be withheld

yod—tenth letter of the 22 letter Hebrew alphabet with a numerical value of ten. It is the first letter of the name of G-d and the upper tip of the *yod* points toward *Keter*.

yovel—jubilee

zayin—seventh letter of the 22 letter Hebrew alphabet with a numerical value of seven

ze'eir anpin—short tempered

zekhut—merit

zizit—variation of *tsitsit* or *tzitzit*

zohama—filth or slime, lust

Zohar—radiance

Lightning Source UK Ltd.
Milton Keynes UK
UKHW03f1849220418
321474UK00001B/125/P